S. H. M. (Samuel Hawkins Marshall) Byers

What i Saw in Dixie Or Sixteen Months in Rebel Prisons

S. H. M. (Samuel Hawkins Marshall) Byers

What i Saw in Dixie Or Sixteen Months in Rebel Prisons

ISBN/EAN: 9783742817396

Manufactured in Europe, USA, Canada, Australia, Japa

Cover: Foto ©Thomas Meinert / pixelio.de

Manufactured and distributed by brebook publishing software
(www.brebook.com)

S. H. M. (Samuel Hawkins Marshall) Byers

What i Saw in Dixie Or Sixteen Months in Rebel Prisons

.

What I Saw in Dixie;

—OR—

SIXTEEN MONTHS

In Rebel Prisons.

BY ADJUTANT S. H. M. BYERS.

DANSVILLE, NEW-YORK:
ROBBINS & POORE, PRINTERS, EXPRESS PRINTING HOUSE.
1868.

DEDICATION.

I gratefully dedicate this little Story of my Prison life to

EDWARD EDWARDS,

The old Slave, of Columbia, South Carolina, who aided me in my escape to Freedom.

Our chains fell off together, and I would not now ask a privilege or right from my Country that I would not willingly accord to him.

THE AUTHOR.

TO THE READER.

—◆—

THIS note is not written to ask the Critic to spare his stereotyped criticism upon my unpolished Story, nor yet to apologize to Rebels for having written the same; but simply to say that the work would have appeared long ago had not continued illness — the result of imprisonment — forbade the labor necessary to prepare it for the press.

The narrative is mostly an extension of my diary, kept in prison, while many of the pages are extracts, *verbatim*, from the diary, as written and afterwards brought through the lines by myself. It is not a story of what others said, or heard, or saw; but incidents that occurred under my own observation, and, incredible as it may seem, the half has not been told. Nor can I be accused of printing these pages to stir anew the smouldering flames that would fain consume the perpetrators of these hellish crimes, for while outrage and murder of loyal citizens continue in the South, our Nation will not readily forget her fourteen thousand murdered sons who sleep, uncoffined, at Andersonville alone,—nor yet her thousands of human wrecks who walk our land—the victims of Southern cruelty and hate.

CONTENTS.

CHAPTER I.

VICKSBURG was ours! We had celebrated the Fourth
of July, 1863, by receiving the arms and banners of thirty
thousand Rebels, who looked on in amazement while we
planted our colors on the old Court House, in the City, and
sang : "*Rally 'round the Flag, Boys!*"

My regiment, the gallant Fifth Iowa, was reposing on its
laurels — well-earned by many a march and hard-fought battle. We were on duty as Post Guards; pleasant duty, but not
to last.

The summer was passing away, and battles were being
lost and won. Rosencrans and Bragg met like two tornadoes
at Chickamauga, and, after a terrible battle, our forces were
compelled to fall back to Chattanooga, — a town on the Tennessee river, and under Lookout Mountain.

Here, in the mud and rain, — hungry, dispirited and defeated, lay the grand army of the Cumberland. What was to
be done! Some one had blundered, and our Cause seemed to
be in the ebb. By the middle of October, 1863, our camp was
in an uproar. News had come! Grant had superseded

Rosencrans, and orders had come for Sherman to take his corps — twenty-five thousand strong — up the river to Memphis, and then march to Grant, at Chattanooga. With the promptness peculiar to that accomplished soldier, Sherman soon had us on board the boats, and moving up to Memphis.— Then commenced a long and weary march, through the enemy's country; but our boys were old soldiers — bearing their scars from many a hard-fought field.

By the 22d of November the march was done, and we were placed on the left of the grand army fronting the rebel hosts, securely posted on Lookout Mountain and Mission Ridge. Our army now numbered near one hundred thousand men, and Grant was our leader. The rebel army was nearly as strong, and commanded by Lt. Gen'l Bragg.

The battle commenced on the 22d inst., near Lookout Mountain, in front of Joe Hooker. On the evening of the 23d Gen. Thomas, commanding the centre of our army, moved forward one mile, and captured the rifle pits of the enemy, after two hours of artillery and musketry practice. At 3 o'clock on the morning of the 23d, (November), our corps, consisting of five Divisions, commenced crossing the Tennessee in pontoon boats. The enemy was on the opposite bank, and we could not put down the pontoon bridge. It was very dark, and the first regiment over the river captured the pickets of the enemy without firing a gun. It was a strange spectacle; an army rowing across a wide and rapid river — and that in the front of a powerful enemy — into whose hands the darkness might betray us; but Sherman was our leader, and not a heart faltered.

By daylight we were well over, and our flags floated to the breeze on the hills, and in the valleys adjoining "Mission

Ridge"—one of the strongest positions ever held by an army.

The morning of the 25th was clear and warm; one of those beautiful Autumnal days so common in the South. The first part of the day was spent in gaining position which was attended by heavy and continued skirmishing. By 12 M. Sherman was ordered to advance and storm the mountain in his front, and attack the enemy's right wing, under Hardee.— It was a desperate undertaking; but it was the order, and we moved.

The advance was made in fine style, under a heavy storm of shot and shell. It seemed as if every foot of the valley was swept by the Rebel Batteries, securely posted along the mountain.

"Forward, boys! Double-quick,—Steady, Charge!"— and away we dashed through the leaden storm of bullets, that grew thicker and fiercer as we advanced.

> ——"Oh, it was grand!
> Like the tempest we charged, in the triumph to share—
> The tempest—its fury and thunder were there;
> On, on o'er entrenchments, o'er living and dead—
> With the Foe under foot, and our Flag overhead!
> Oh, it was grand!"

The valley was crossed, and we were at the bottom of the mountain. Many had already fallen, and now we were met by double lines of Rebels, who were coming down the mountain-side like an avalanche. It was too much; our Brigade was temporarily repulsed, our leader—the brave Gen. Matthies—and a host of other gallant officers, were shot; but the boys rallied, and the rebel lines were pierced at six different points. Over the mountain we charged — the day was ours — and the "back-bone of the rebellion was broken."

It was in the first charge on the face of the mountain that eighty of my regiment, including myself, were captured. — I was then near the mouth of the tunnel that ran under the mountain. The first line of rebels dashed down by me, shooting my wounded and retreating comrades. I was now between two lines of the enemy, and among the rocks. I picked up a copy of Bonner's *Ledger*, which one of the boys had dropped, and waved it in token of my surrender; but they "didn't read the Ledger," and fired on me immediately. I then ran down toward the line below me; but I was a "goner!"

"You Yankee son of a —— ! come out of that sword, and run to the top of the hill, or we will blow you to h—l!" exclaimed one of the "gray-coats."

I did not stop to argue the point then, but marched at the point of a bayonet to the top of the mountain.

By this time our lines had rallied, and were coming with a yell.

The day was ours, but I was a prisoner in the hands of a more than barbarous foe. In a hollow behind the mountain I found the remainder of my captive comrades. There were eighty of my own regiment, of whom only *sixteen* lived to return from prison.

We were at once put on the retreating march, for the camp-fires of the "yankees" blazed on the mountain behind us, and we could hear the glad cries of victory. We were taken back to the Chickamauga battle-field — given a few crackers, and ordered to march all night.

The battle of Chickamauga was fought a month previous, yet the Union dead were still unburied; as we were marched by the field we were tauntingly told that "If we could not see our dead brothers on the field, we could at least smell them."

CHAPTER II.

"From here to Kingston, Georgia, is eighty miles, and you must walk there rapidly as possible;" said the rebel, Captain Mace, who had charge of us. And so we started down the railroad — walking on the ties — with a line of saucy rebels on each side of us.

I had scarcely slept for a week; and now, tired and hungry, I must walk all night. But I slept some; yes, strange as it may seem, I would sleep as I walked, — and if we stopped for a few moments' rest, nothing but kicks and curses would compel us to start again.

Daylight came, when we had a short rest, near the town of Ringold. By 9 o'clock we were again on the march, and were in Dalton by dark. Here we would have had a few hours' rest; but the "yankee army" was coming, a hundred thousand strong; and the "rebs," not liking the growl of Sherman's "dogs of war," moved on quietly, but rapidly.

At noon of the 28th, we passed the fortified town of Resacca, on the Chatahoochie river. Here some of us were again searched and robbed. Lt. O'Brien, of St. Louis, asked to be

SIXTEEN MONTHS IN REBEL PRISONS. 7

allowed to keep his fine comb. "No," said the chivalrous rebel, "you can go lousy, damn you!"

On we went to Calhoun, where we received some crackers; then we marched to near Kingston, and camped in the woods. The night was cold and windy, so we could not sleep. They marched some rebel "deserters," as they called them, with us; but they were loyal Tennesseeans, and would not fight, so they were chained in couples and were now on their way to the prison; or, more likely, the gallows. *

November 30th was cold and dreary; we were placed in dirty stock-cars, and started for Atlanta. At dark we passed Marietta,—the home of Stevens, Vice President of the Confederate States. The prisoners huddled together, and kept warm; but two of the guards froze to death, on top of the train.

Before midnight we were in Atlanta, and remained in a cold, dark pen, without any fire, until the next day.

December 1st was spent in Atlanta. Here we met two of our officers, who had been in chains for months, for some trifling offence.

From Atlanta we were taken to Augusta, on the Savannah river. The town is beautiful—the river dark and muddy. The people are not rejoicing over recent battles, as their wounded sons and brothers are now coming in by the car-load. There is a great rush among men, women and children, to see the "hated yankees." Barnum, with all his monkeys and bears, could never draw such crowds of inquisitors as we have here.

In the evening we cross the river, and tread our "hireling" feet upon the sacred soil of South Carolina. Away we

* I have since learned that these men were shot.

go for the Capital of the State, and by daylight we are again
on exhibition; this is the finest town with the most heartless
people I have seen in Dixie. We were taken through the
streets, and received the jeers, taunts and curses, of a bitter
enemy.

Here they changed us to cars, dirtier, and crowded still
worse than before; yet this was in the Capital of South Carolina, and we were in the hands of the Palmetto Chivalry.—
We bore their insults in silence, but did not forget them. Afterwards, when I had escaped, I saw them in their grief; I saw
their city burn to ashes, and their proud spirits laid low in the
dust. Their great men were fallen, and their proud men were
beggars; then I could not but recall to mind the bitter senti-
ments of Byron, so strongly poured forth in Mazeppa.

> " We paid them well in after days —
> There was not of their castle — gate,
> Stone, bar, moat, bridge or barrier left ;
> I saw their turrets in a blaze —
> Their crackling battlements all cleft !
> And the hot lead pour down, like rain
> From off the scorched and blackening roof,
> Whose thickness was not vengeance-proof.
> They little thought that day of pain,
> When launched, as on the lightning's flash,
> They bade us to destruction dash !
> That one day we should come again
> With twice five thousand men,
> To thank them for their uncourteous ride.
> But time at last sets all things even —
> And if we do but watch the hour,
> There never yet was human power
> Which could evade, if unforgiven,
> The patient search and vigil long,
> Of him who treasures up a wrong."

1 *

By the 6th of December we were in Raleigh, the Capital of North Carolina. We were treated peaceably and decently at this city. From Raleigh we were hurried on to Weldon, N. C., where we halted for one day, and were allowed to buy our dinner at a little tavern. Bill of fare: corn-bread, turnips, potatoes and tough beef, for which we paid three dollars each. Here we exchanged what few "greenbacks" we had managed to hide when first robbed, for Confederate notes, at the rate of five for one.

From Weldon we went to Richmond, via. Petersburg; the latter place we reached at midnight. Here we slept in the cars till morning, then entered the Capital of "the Confederate States of America! Big title, big city, big chivalry! Over the long bridge we go. Down below, almost under us, is "Belle Isle," with its five thousand prisoners, shivering in the cold wind from the river James.

Halt! What building is this, so much like a ware-house? It is the famous "Libby Prison."

Maj. Thomas P. Turner, in command, comes forward and says:

"Gentlemen, it becomes my duty to relieve you of all money and valuables in your possession, before you enter the prison."

We demurred; no use—

"Fork it out, or be chained in the dungeon."

A few had money in the soles of their boots; some had it in their mouths, and thus saved it. But we passed muster, and were told to march up stairs; the door swung to, and we were "fresh-fish" in Libby. Now commenced the initiatory ceremonies by the older prisoners. "Fresh-fish!" "Fresh-fish!" "Don't touch him!" "Who aren't lousy!" "Put him in

pickle!"   "Give 'em the 'bill of fare!'"   "Where's your
sword—who thinks he has a nice thing of it!"   "Who wants
rations—who likes copperheads!"

"Fresh-fish, fresh-fish!" was the astonishing reply given
in a loud voice, at the other end of the room, to each of these,
and a hundred other, strange queries.

But in an hour's time we had shaken hands all around,
said "how d'ye do," and told the news from "God's land,"
to unlucky representatives from almost every State in the
Union.

Maine was there,— Minnesota, California, and even North
Carolina.   We all shook hands, and rejoiced that, though we
were in prison, a million more were ready and willing to take
our places, and plant the flag even in the city of Richmond,
and over the walls of "Libby Prison."

CHAPTER III.

Most prisons are lonesome, dark and quiet. Not so with Libby; for there are six hundred officers huddled together here, and sometimes the confusion makes it a second Babel. There is no glass in the windows, hence we have light for the present, and for that matter, air, too.

The prison stands on the James river, with the Kanawha canal between. It is three stories high. The upper rooms are used for prisoners; the lower for officers and guards. It was formerly a ship-chandler's store-room, and owned by Libby & Son; hence its name.

This is my second day in prison, and I have been around the "city" of Libby; (for its bustle and noise resemble a city in-doors.) I have not met one familiar face yet; but there is a splendid opportunity for extending one's acquaintance. I am placed in the upper, east room; each group of half a dozen has a temporary table made from old boxes, which answers at once for table, cupboard and wardrobe. When night comes the seats etc., are piled on top of the tables, and they stretch out upon the floor to sleep, to dream,

perchance, of battle-fields; or, what is sweeter, home and kin-
dred friends. When morning comes the blankets are rolled
up, the corn-bread is disposed of, and then commences another
day of painful anxiety and hope deferred. For weeks and
months they have been hoping and expecting exchange, or
something that would release them from suffering.

An occasional paper from the North finds its way into
the prison, and from one of these I learn that I was killed (?)
at one of the recent battles. Gratifying intelligence, truly!
But I am convinced of the untruthfulness of the statement,
having just pinched myself, and find that it is I, and that I
"still live!"

To-day I wrote some letters home, which I expect to send
North by flag of truce. These truce-boats meet in the James
river, near Fort Darling. By them we receive an occasional
line from the North.

We received a few boxes of clothing, etc., to-day, from
the Sanitary Commissions in the North. God bless them for
it! In some of the pockets and stockings, letters were found,
written by the fair hands that made them. These letters
contained sweet words of sympathy and encouragement.
Oh! fair and stranger writer, you little know what a heal-
ing balm you put upon our bleeding wounds. We know,
now, that we are not forgotten,—and that the woman of the
North are true-hearted and loyal. God bless them all.

We are not all idle here. Every group of four or five is
at something to help pass away the time that drags so drearily
along. For amusement, if for nothing else, I will note the
manner in which the different groups are engaged at the present moment.

Party number one, reading a magazine; No. two, playing

cards; No. three, discussing the propriety of arming negroes; No. four, reading; No. five, playing the violin; No. six, cards; No. seven, reciting in Latin; No. eight, playing back-gammon; No. nine, at chess; No. ten; writing a diary; No. eleven, smoking; No. twelve, reading the Bible; No's thirteen and fourteen, making bone rings to sell for rations, or to carry home as "relics of 'modern barbarism!'" Among the prisoners are fine singers and musicians. Some money has been raised, and a few instruments purchased; so that now we have a string band, and at times Libby presents occasions as merry as a marriage bell. But this is the bright side of prison life, that is shaded by long and wearisome days, the thoughts of home and liberty, and above all, the iron bars and frowning sentinels, that seem to say: "Stand back; you have no freedom now."

With four others—Capt's Page and Bascom, Lieut's Austin and Hoffman—I am located in the upper, east room. At a table near my left is a son of Admiral Paulding—a noble young man and a fighting patriot. Near our right is Brig. Gen. Neal Dow—the great temperance reformer, and originator of the "Maine Liquor Law." Intemperance seems to worry him but little, here, as he spends most of his time playing chess or reading. He is a small, gray-haired man, with gray eyes; is an agreeable speaker, and is much respected by all who know him in prison. A good joke is told of him, which afterwards appeared in the "drawer" of *Harper's Weekly.*—The prison abounded in vermin, and nothing but continued "skirmishing," as we called it, would keep them at bay. One morning the General, with back and shoulders in a state of nudity, was sitting by the light busily hunting the seams of his old, red shirt. An officer approaching, said:

"What, General! you are not lousy I hope."

"No," replied the General; "*But my shirt is!*"

The 15th of December was a cold day in prison, but we kept warm by dancing, jumping, etc. A flag of truce goes North, and I send the following "piece of silliness" to my old friend, Will. Edmundson.

> Well, William! my boy, 'tis in prison, I thank ye:
>   They've got me, at last, just for being a "yankee!"
> And waiting, I am, for the paps to arrange
>   That beautiful system they call "an exchange"—
> And while I am waiting, this letter I'll send
>   By the first flag of truce—the poor yankee's friend.
> I am well—what more could a prisoner wish!
>   Unless women and wine could be served in one dish!
> 'Twas a very warm time, Will, the day of the "spree,"
>   When they nabbed us, and brought us up here—do you see!
> 'Twas a dodging of grape-shot and dodging of shell—
>   And I thought, once or twice, we were all gone to ——
>   Thunder without any sail!
>   'Till the smoke cleared away, and we landed in Jall.

A few boxes of provisions are being received, by those who sent for them months ago. Before delivering them, however, the rebels subject them to a close search, to discover whether they may not contain greenbacks or other contrabands of war. Cans of fruit are bursted open and probed with a stick—the same stick being used in all cans, whether of pickles or salt. Cheese is split open, bottles emptied, and packages all torn loose and contents emptied, in search of Uncle Sam's almighty Dollar; which, if found, is claimed by the chivalry as their property, we suppose by right of discovery.

All new prisoners are called "fresh-fish;" and I now know what they meant by yelling fresh-fish so lustily when we came in on the 8th.

Weather out-doors is said to be quite cool; and there is no over-heating in old Libby.

I am reciting in Latin to Maj. Marshall, of the 5th Iowa. I progress favorably considering it is mostly done on an empty stomach.

Our dinner to-day consisted of corn-bread dried beef and water; but we don't complain if it will only hold out at this. Greenbacks are not allowed in prison, yet the city brokers will give five ".Confeds" for one of Uncle Sam's notes at any time.

One of the prisoners executed an excellent counterfeit five-dollar bill with a steal pen. He traded it for Confederate notes, and lived better for a week.

The following is the price-list of provisions in the city for this week, copied from a rebel paper. Bacon, $3,00 per pound; potatoes, $18,00 per bushel; turkeys, $25,00 each; sugar, $3;50 per pound; beef, $1,00 per pound; butter, $5,00 per pound; whiskey, $75,00 per gallon.

Captains Sawyer and Flynn—both of whom were sentenced to be hung, in retaliation for the hanging of two spies, by Burnside—are among the prisoners. Sawyer is a German, from Cape Island, New-Jersey. The day had been appointed for his death, and permission granted to his wife to come and see him before he was hung. On the appointed day, she came as far as the rebel lines, but they refused to pass her further; with a heavy, almost broken heart, she returned to her home. For some reason the execution was postponed indefinitely; and the two officers now live in terrible anxiety of mind.

Col. Straight is confined in the dungeon, under Libby, for endeavoring to effect his escape.

This part of Dixie is much disturbed, just now, by a

yankee by the name of Averill,—who is racing over the country, tearing up railroads and carrying fear to the hearts of
many of Virginia's chivalry.

Rumors of exchange of prisoners are current in the prison, and all are rejoicing in the prospects of speedy release.
Vain hope! Glorious expectations, but seldom realized. No
mail, and not a word from home; have they forgotten us?

Christmas in prison! The day is cold and gloomy; wo
have but little fuel for fire, so comfort is out of the question.
I am thinking of the bright and happy firesides, to-day, in the
far-off North. In my imagination I see the over-joyed faces;
the parties; the balls; and hear the ringing of the merry,
merry bells. Oh! the hearts full of joy; the laughing girls
and boys, who wish that "Christmas might last all the year."
Happy, joyous ones, I would not mar your enjoyment by
having you, for a moment, think, to-day, of your friends in the
dungeons of the South. In the evening I wrote the following
lines, and inscribed them to Capt. Sawyer, who is under sen-
tence of death.

IN LIBBY.

Alone, alone ; how dark and drear
    Is life within this prison cell ;
My cold, damp couch seems but a bier —
    My very voice a funeral knell
That sadly tolls, amid my pains,
In mockery of these iron chains.

I hear the music of the bells
    Float out upon the Southern air :
Now like the sea their chorus swells,
    Now faintly as the breath of prayer —
Yet, lingering still, as if to bless
My heart within its loneliness.

The tide comes up from out the bay —
 The sails ride to and fro ;
I stand and watch them all the day,
 Out on the stream below.
But bending sail, nor flowing sea,
Brings one sweet word of joy to me.

For treason taints the soft South air,
 And orphans cry aloud for bread ;
While murder, stalking everywhere,
 Laughs o'er its own unburied dead,
Till Hell seems bursting all aflame,
And Freedom hides her face in shame.

Oh ! strike again, ye marshal'd hosts,
 Who draw the sword for Liberty ;
For now, the hated tyrant boasts,
 This land shall bow to Slavery.
And yonder, where the blue cross waves,
Goes up the shout " *Ye, too, are slaves !* "

Let not the Past be all in vain,
 Nor pause to soothe thy widowed sorrow ;
Thy heroes sleep upon the plain,
 And glory waits thee on the morrow.
For God will hold the freeman's hand,
And guide thee well, my own proud land.

During the past week a few hundred prisoners, from Belle
Isle, were sent North ; so we, in Libby, are hoping for exchange. Maj. Gen. Butler is now appointed Commissioner of
Exchange, so we look for something to be done. But no ! He
is scarcely appointed before the Rebel Government refuses to
acknowledge him ; pronounces him an "out-law" and a beast,
—not entitled to the rights of a man or a soldier. So we are
disappointed; and "exchange" is "below par !"

We have just heard of the great prize-fight, in England,

between Heenan and King, in which Heenan was whipped.—
Glad of it! This may put an end to some of the notorious
bragging, for which the yankee "fancy" is becoming famous.

Many of the prisoners now occupy the time in making
rings, watch-seals, bodkins etc., of beef-bones; and the many
articles that are daily whittled out, would do credit to a fan-
cy-store, on Broadway.

Only an occasional prisoner gives up to grim despair; he
grows melancholy, weak and careless; finally, he sickens and
dies. His remains are taken out and buried, we know not
how or where,—we never being allowed to assist at the funer-
al of any one.

December 31st, 11 o'clock at night! The old year is almost gone. We have been allowed to keep lights burning in
the prison later, to-night, than usual. I have spent the day,
and thus far the night, in reading the "*Unionist's Daughter*"—
a history of many of the thrilling events occurring in Tennessee. What those loyal, suffering people have endured, God
only knows. It costs Northern men comparatively little to be
true to their country, but the loyal Southerner buys his prin-
ciples and love of country, at the sacrifice of friends, property,
home, and often life itself.

I learn by the rebel papers that thousands of the Union
men of East Tennessee are fugitives in the mountains; and are
"hunted down like wild beasts." Let the rebel persecutors be-
ware! There is a dread future yet to come; the lane is long
that has no turn, and Fortune's wheel is still moving. Might
will not always triumph over Right. Freedom will yet assert
her own, even in the dark and dreary mountains of the South.
Truth is there, and sooner or later Vengeance will come, fol-

lowed by the burning homes and broken hearts of a, widowed State.

We commence the new year this morning, with cold weather, and the "meal-barrel almost empty!" There is nothing we can do whereby to warm ourselves, unless it be— pounding, scuffling, or dancing a jig to the cold winds that whistle through our open windows, from the river James. At It we go: "balance all—swing partners;" but it is a "Stag-dance" after all—and there's no fun, so we give that up.— "A song for the New Year!" Capt. Mass—the funny "Ham-fat-man—sings his funniest song, and we all join in the "cho-rus." Bless us! What harmony; what concord of sweet sounds. "Kingdom Coming," and "John Brown," where are you? Such a welcome to the New-Year never went up from prison-house before. "On with the dance; let joy be uncon-fined!" and again the old floor quakes with the tramping troopers, as they dash up and down the room, in waltz, polka or quadrille.

Night comes at last, and the boys "turn in." Not to sumptuous couch, with downy pillows, but to a single blanket —upon a dirty floor—to sleep, perchance to dream.

The Rebel Congress is now in session in Richmond, and is dire and doleful in its attempts to peg up the Rebellion, that now seems to be in the wane. Some of its prominent leaders are fast losing faith. All appear to feel that treason and re-bellion must soon cease, unless Fate sends some unlooked for relief. At present they are resolving in favor of wholesale con-scription, of every man and boy in the South—willing or un-willing. Others, still more desperate, cry out: "Arm the slaves! They will fight our battles for us;" while "cuffy" grins, and says: "Yes, massa! jest arm us, and you'll see what dis chile will do. Yes, massa! we fight—fight berry hard!" and his eyes glow with the hope that he may yet bo able to strike a blow for himself. But the rebels are a little chary of their "faithful servants" as they call them. The darkey could and would fight; but on which side was a ques- tion filled, to them, with uncertainties.

How we, in prison, hoped that they would arm the slaves, and place them over us, instead of the miserable rascals and villians, who now boast their intentions to have "yankee scalps."

"Money, or no money." "Pay our debts, or not pay them." These are questions now vexing the South, and the probability is that they will be answered by measures even worse than repudiation. Paper currency is poorly executed on an inferior quality of paper, and the result is that millions of dollars in counterfeit notes are now floating over the South. No attention, scarcely, is paid to the apperance of notes, and thus a counterfeit passes as readily as good money.

The people are going wild over the finances. Exorbitant prices are demanded for everything. Five hundred dollars are asked for a pair of boots, and every thing else in proportion.

It is a criminal offence to deal in U. S. notes or bonds, yet hundreds are speculating with them on the "sly." The knowing ones are converting their effects into Uncle Sam's Treasury notes, and laying them by for a "rainy day"—when the "boys in blue" come marching along.

The rebel raider, John Morgan, has escaped from the Ohio Penitentiary, and to-day came into Libby to pay us a visit. He is a rakish-looking chap, but is gentlemanly for all that. He spoke kindly to us, and appeared to sympa-

thize with us in our misfortune; remarking that "the South
was being disgraced by its cruel treatment of prisoners."

The military and citizens turned out *en masse*, and gave
him a reception as the "Marion" of the South.

The weather is very cold, and several of the poor fellows
on Belle Isle froze to death last night,—while hundreds of the
poorer families in Richmond are suffering for want of the most
common necessaries of life.

Brig. Gen. Neal Dow, who is a prisoner here, gave us a
lecture, last evening, on temperance. It was full of interest,
and delivered in a manner well worthy the reputation of its
author. The General's principle is to punish the rum-seller,
and not his victim—the drunkard. The reformation following
the prohibition of rum-selling in Maine and other New-Eng-
land States, proves the correctness of this principle.

Neal Dow's style of speaking is neither strange or peculiar; he does not possess the qualities of a loud declaimer, or
the tricky comedian—so common to temperance lecturers.—
His voice is soft and clear, and the words flow with an ease almost beyond conception. His arguments are solid and original—interspersed with an occasional pleasantry—that makes
his manner extremely agreeable. Some of the rebel officers
came in, and listened to the lecture; but thought it a poor affair, no doubt, as it came from a loyal man.

"Hurrah! hurrah!" exclaimed some of the boys; "there's
our boxes from home, and all full of good things!" And so
it was; there was the schooner—laden with boxes for the prisoners—and thus expectations for "good things" ran high; eagerly we watched, and patiently we waited. Days passed; a
few of the boxes were sent in—others were stolen by the
guards; finally, wholesale confiscation took the place of petty

stealing—all that remained being sent to the rebel hospitals—
and we may still go hungry.

It seems to be the policy of our captors to give us as little
food as possible themselves and allow none from our friends in
the North, who are willing and anxious to relieve us.

A mail has been received, but we have no letters until
they have been inspected by the prison authorities.

It is now the last of January. Without, the weather
seems delightful,—which renders life in this dark and crowded
pen almost unendurable.

The rations at present are really horrible. They consist
of only a *little half-baked corn-bread,-and a gill or two of rice.*
"Moderate" diet, truly. Some of the officers, who have money,
ey, purchase a little flour—at the modest rate of eight dollars
por pound. What a contrast between the ration given to the
rebel prisoners, in the North, and the miserable, half-cooked
stuff, eked out to Northern prisoners, here in the South.

·Below is a list of provisions, received by the rebel prisoners at Rock Island, Elmyra, and at other prisons in the North,
in accordance with Government orders.

   Pork or Beef,
   Flour or Bread,
   Beans,
   Rice,
   Potatoes, (desiccated)
   Vegetables, (mixed)
   Sugar,
   Salt,
   Vinegar, and
   Coffee.

And all of these, too, in abundant quantities, and of the best quality. Truly, Uncle Sam furnishes food fit for the gods,—when compared with Libby rations.

Last night three of the inmates of Belle Isle made a futile effort to escape, and were shot—one of them seven times. There are now six thousand on the Island, and near one thousand here; officers, only, are confined in Libby. We are crowded almost to death—all sleeping upon the floor. It seems as though my "board" grows harder every night. The boys on the Island have had no meat for eleven days, and now kill, cook and eat every dog that has the "misfortune" to stray within the prison lines: yet Pollard—editor of the Richmond *Examiner*—in an article this morning, says: "*That's right; it is 'dog eat dog!'*" Oh, chivalry! where is thy shame?

There are now nine hundred of the prisoners sick in the hospital. To-day the "Johnies" are placing iron bars over every window—giving Libby the appearance of a Penitentiary.

The first month of the new year has slipped by, and I am still a prisoner—waiting and watching for something to "turn up," as the phrase goes, but there seems little, favorable, in the signs of the times. So I pet my patience, and wait. Now-a-days Libby is rather quiet, save when an officer attempts his escape, when, if detected, he is chained in the dungeon, under the prison.

As we have but little to eat we are seldom troubled with "night-mare;" but on the contrary our dreams are usually sweet. Last night was cold again, and notwithstanding I had but a single blanket for bedding, and the "hard side" of a board for a couch, my dreams were uncommonly sweet.

> I kissed thee, last night, in my dreams, Sue!
> And thy blushes but made thee more fair;
> Oh! sweet are the realms of sleep, Sue,
> When thou art the empress there.

Sunday, Feb. 9th.—All Richmond is in an uproar, to-day, as the Federal troops are advancing on the city, from the Peninsula. The bells are ringing the wild alarm, and the streets are jammed with the excited mob; some expecting to defend the city and others to plunder it. It is confidently assert-ed that the yankees are coming to burn the Capital and release the prisoners confined here. Extraordinary precautions are taken to prevent any disposition on our part to mutiny. How-itzers are dragged through the streets, and brought to bear on the prison and the bridges over the river James. Old men and little boys have rushed to arms, and the fortifications of the city are filled with the veteran soldiery, the raw militia and the frightened citizens.

All day the bells rang, and the people ran to and fro; not till darkness had veiled the city did the tumult cease, and then but few sought repose,—for no one knew at what moment the terrible "yanks" might come upon them, and visit just vengeance on the long threatened city.

To us poor fellows, in prison, the excitement was amusing; all we could do was to peep through our grated windows, and laugh at the ridiculousness of the whole affair. Who could have believed that the pretended Capital of a Nation could be thrown into such a frantic uproar by a raiding party of seven thousand men? Not till noon of the next day did the city re-sume its senses—at that time, as the "rebs" say, Richmond being "safe" again.

As the people of Richmond had their excitement, on Sun-day, so we, of the *Hotel de Libby*, had ours on Tuesday night last. For several weeks past, two of the prisoners had been engaged in digging a tunnel from the bottom of the fire-place, in the kitchen, under the walls and feet of the guards, who

stood around the prison, and twelve feet from it, thence to
the rear of a ware-house, across the street. The whole affair had been kept secret with a chosen few, and was completed on the above night; then commenced an exodus of
captives, which continued until one hundred and nine had
escaped, and were fast making their way to "Abraham's
bosom."

Daylight, only, prevented the escape of all in the prison.
The morning roll-call revealed the condition of affairs, and
scouts were immediately sent, in every direction, to re-cap-
ture the fugitives. Dispatches were sent to all parts of the
rebel lines surrounding the city, but all in vain; only twen-
twenty-five of the escaped were found, and they were sent to
the dungeon below.

A few of the prisoners, it is said, were dogged down; and
refusing to surrender, were shot.

The time consumed in digging the tunnel was forty-six
nights. The distance was eighty feet. Five foundations of
solid rock were passed, and the route was under the feet of the
sentinels guarding the prison.

Bishop Johns, of Richmond, has spoken to the Libbyites
a time or two; he is a good speaker.

Weather is quite cool, and many of us suffer, at night, for
want of blankets.

A flag of truce boat is up the river to-day, again, and we
have a few Northern papers and letters; so we can have some
good cheer, at least, in reading how the old flag floats in
the northern breeze.

Another month is gone; the weather has moderated, and
all out-doors seems full of loveliness. Our prison is dark and
gloomy—in strange contrast with the bright sunshine and pure

air, outside—that almost tempts us to break through our bars, knock down the guards—and breathe, for a time at least, the pure air of heaven.

We are allowed to write one letter a week, but are limited to six lines; short and sweet.

To-day the rebels capped the climax of their inhumanity by reading the following order: "Hereafter all clothing hung near or outside the windows, will be confiscated; *and officers standing near the windows will be liable to be shot!*"

A prisoner enquired of Maj. Turner, who read the order, "what he meant by 'near the windows;' what distance."

Turner replied: "Damn you, keep away from the windows entirely!"

Thus we are now debarred of even the poor privilege of looking through our barred windows. Cruel wretches! man may forget you, but God will give you justice.

To-day, (March 23d,) the rebels killed one of their own officers, through mistake. He was in the lower prison on duty, and put his head out at the window to speak to a sentinel; the sentinel, thinking he was a yankee prisoner, obeyed the above order—shooting him dead. So their hellishness begins on their own head, to the result of which we all say—amen.

General Kilpatrick is now racing around the city, and fighting rebels wherever he can find them. The citizens' home-guards and soldiers, are all armed, and fighting the bold raiders, who they fear will release the prisoners and burn the city. The bells ring, and everybody is excited. Last evening they came so close to the city that we could hear the musketry.

Many of the hopeful expect the city to be taken, and the prisoners freed. We are all organized in Companies—ready to aid should the city fall.

It is positively asserted by negroes, who assisted, that Turner has placed several kegs of powder under the prison, and will blow us up should the city be taken.

A number of the prisoners captured from Kilpatrick have been brought in, and confined in a pen with negroes. Col. Dalgreen was killed, and his mutilated body exposed, in the city, to the gaze of the rabble.

The papers say that the authorities will bury the body where nothing short of the last trump will find it. So they fear even the poor, dead body of a fallen foe.

Capt. Hammond had his ear partly shot off, this evening, by a guard, who fired on him as he stood in front of an opening in the sink.

So it goes. We are in constant danger of losing our lives, as there is no telling when a sentinel may feel himself affronted and fire into the room, as instructed by Maj Thomas P. Turner, commanding Libby. This man is a fiend; and sooner than he suspects, may receive a fiend's deserts. Might will not always trample over Right, nor will the thousand wrongs practiced upon helpless prisoners go unavenged.

The Rebel Journals are crying loudly for the Black flag, and the hanging of every Northern man caught upon Southern soil.

"Extermination" is their motto, now while they are safe; but let the tables turn, and they will sing an entirely different song.

Marshal Kane, of Baltimore, a notorious rebel, visited the prison, to-day. His treasonable conduct in the North caused his arrest and confinement in Fort McHenry. After his release he ran the blockade, and came to Richmond—where he is lionized as a martyr. He is now appointed to the

command of all Marylanders in Dixie. His command is to
be styled "The Maryland Line"—composed, principally, of
Renegades like himself. *. ‌

On the 20th of March about one thousand rebels wero
sent down from the North, to be exchanged. All Richmond
was out to give them a grand reception. Cannons boomed,
and sweet music floated on the air. The prisoners were received from the vessel, and with an escort of soldiers and citizens, marched into the city—where hot coffee, and speeches
from the Governor and Jeff. Davis, were served up, in true
Dixie style.

The officers in Libby, anxious to see the cavalcade, of
course, as it passed the prison, crowded up to the windows; for
this temerity one of them was shot in the head, by a rebel sentinel. Others had narrow escapes from being shot—myself
being among the number. A sentinel had "drawn a bead" on
me, and was about to fire ; when a fellow-prisoner happened to
see him, and pulled me back from the window.   •   •

When we first came to Libby we found a number here,
who were soft-gloved and copperish, toward the rebs.   They
were disciples of that dastardly and treasonable sheet—the
Chicago *Times*. A few weeks here, however, converted them
to the true faith; and knocked the scales from their eyes.—
The Chicago *Times* is below par here, now, although some of
the most bitter and treasonable articles to be found in the rebel papers, are extracts from its columns.

March 28th, 1864. The prison, to-day, is dark and
gloomy.   Out-doors is full of cold and rain ; yet the little
bare-footed boys and girls, of the city of Richmond, stand in
the streets, all day, to pick up the miserable crumbs, thrown
out of the windows—carrying them home to their starving

mothers—"who have not had," say the morning papers, "either bread or fuel, during the last three days of cold and storm."

Richmond is full of paupers, widows and orphans, whose cries of want fall on pitiless ears. The rich leaders of the rebellion revel in splendor, and cruelly curse those whom their wicked treachery has impoverished; and all this in the Capital, and under the very eyes of the Government of the so-called Confederate States of America.

One of the privates, who was in prison across the street, was killed by a sentinel, for looking out of the window. This hellish outrage, like most others committed here, was by a member of the "City Battalion," or Home guards; men who never saw a battle-field, but remain in Richmond, to strive and murder prisoners of war.

The James river has overflowed its banks, crossed the canal, and is now engaged in drowning rats out of the lower rooms of Libby. A laudable undertaking, and we wish it success.

Our principal amusement, in Libby, is chess-playing; and there are many, here, who excel in the game. To-day our champion, in the East room, sent a challenge to players of the West room. It was accepted, and we were "mated" in a surprisingly short time.

Euchre and back-gammon receive due attention, also, at the hands of some of the boys—many of whom sit with cards in their hands from morning until night. Perhaps it is not a profitable way, but it is at least an easy manner of killing time.

Lt. Forsythe had written to his widowed mother, in Toledo, Ohio, that he expected a "special" exchange, and would be home in a week. This morning he was sitting near the window, reading a novel, when a guard (accidentally, the rebels assert) shot him dead.

We raised some money, purchased a metalic coffin, and sent his dead body to his poor mother, who is waiting in her quiet home, to welcome her dear boy from prison. Ah ! well ; he has gone where there are no more wars, sorrows or troubles. Be comforted, fond mother; your "bread has been cast upon the waters, and after many days ye shall find it."

Three others were wounded by the same shot, but not seriously.

The rebels have at last concluded to recognize Butler—"the beast," as they call him. Whether it will result in any good to us we know not; but live and hope.

All the prisoners from Belle Isle are being sent to Andersonville, where they are huddled in a dirty pen, and are dying by hundreds. The Richmond papers report them dying at the rate of fifty-three per day. It is heart-sickening to think of. Starvation and exposure will soon kill them all.—For this wholesale destruction of life who is responsible but Jeff. Davis, who orders it? The officers here and at Andersonville, are only his puppets, to do his bidding. He cannot plead ignorance, for we have petitioned him for relief; but our petitions have been spurned. Besides, his own papers—published here in his Capital—gloat over the horrors of these prisons, every day. Let us hope that the Justice of God may yet overtake and avenge the wrongs of outraged humanity.

The rebel Journals do little, this Winter, but abuse the North, and boast over their own corruption and what they intend to do in the coming campaign. "When Lee meets Grant

—then comes the tug of war;" so say they, and so say we! and not war's "tug," only, but war's end.

The weather is beautiful, out, now. The fields across the James, are green; the peach trees are in bloom,—and we are allowed the glorious privilege of admiring them, from our prison windows, at the risk of being shot.

The James river is full of fishing boats; these jolly boys sell shad to the citizens of Richmond at the modest figures of $34,00 a pair. Shades of Jonah! where are you?

Libby is filling up rapidly; if this continues until warm weather it will overflow; probably as far as the burying-grounds.

The rebel Congress meets, to-day, for the third, and I hope the last time. Jeff. Davis, in his message, tells them that "the Confederacy is 'all hunk' yet, and that in spite of the 'great humanity' shown to Federal prisoners, they are dying at a 'shocking rate.'"

Is it possible, Mr. Davis! that men who have nothing to eat or wear, will die in spite of your kindness?

May 6th—Our last day in Libby prison. Gen. Grant has crossed the Rapidan, and is fighting the rebels in the Wilderness. At the same time an army is coming up the James river, and threatens the city. Every body is under arms, in Richmond, and hurrying to the front to make another great effort to "save the Capital."

The slaughter on both sides is terrible, and the rebs now call Grant "the butcher."

Richmond is not a safe place for prisoners, so at midnight we are counted and marched out of Libby; for the first time in nearly six months, I breathe the pure air of heaven. Oh, how glorious, how delightful! Libby, farewell; we will not forget you soon; we will remember you even in our dreams; and hope we may yet see you ornamented with the Stars and Stripes.

During the Winter spent in Libby, we had accumulated, from different sources, quite a number of articles,—such as wooden and tin ware, pots, buckets, and all the nice things from home, that had been delivered to us, and saved for a rainy day, or a prison-feast. These the rebels told us we must leave behind, as we could not carry them on the march, which they said we were to make, to Petersburg. We did not know then, as we have since learned, that no orders were issued for a march to Petersburg, but that we would go South on the cars. This strategy was resorted to for the purpose of robbing us of what few comforts we possessed.

CHAPTER IV.

HERE we go, all in cattle-cars—fifty men in a car! Stop a day at Danville, Virginia; are in Barracks No. 4. The rebels look very cheerless, so we guess the tide of battle is in our favor again.

We pass through some of the finest country in the South. Every inch of ground, that can be used to advantage, is planted. Corn everywhere, instead of cotton, as of old.

We pass Augusta, Raleigh and Columbia,—all flourishing towns.

At Augusta the home-guard chivalry turned out, to escort us from one depot to another. Fine fellows, in sparkling uniforms—waving broad swords, and carrying magnificent double-barreled shot-guns at their saddle-bow. They are the merchants and professional men of the city. Judging from their appearance they would make sad havoc were they to encounter a flock of doves.

One of these shot-gun heroes dashed boldly up to one of the prisoners; and, with his blade poised high . in air, threatened to rend him asunder should he again presume to "smile upon the dignity of the occasion."

A son of Governor Brown, of Georgia, was one of the presiding geniuses of the occasion, and bore himself with a pomp and coolness worthy of a Cæsar about to "pass the Rubicon.

Arrived at Macon, we were placed in a sand-pen two acres in extent,—surrounded by a stockade, twelve feet high, on top of which the sentries were placed. Twelve feet inside of the stockade was the *dead-line* ; so called from the fact that any prisoner crossing it would be instantly shot, and without challenge.

Capt. Tabb, who brought us here, returns to Richmond, shortly, and Capt. Gibbs will take his place, in command of the prison.

We have no barracks of any kind, and at present our only shelter from the sun or rain, is our blankets—stretched over pine sticks.

Our rations are still very slim. We are allowed to buy an occasional newspaper, from the sutler, by which we learn reverses have overtaken their army, in the West, and that Richmond is seriously threatened.

At Andersonville, which is some miles below here, the prisoners are still dying by the hundreds.

The weather is beginning to be very warm.

An officer gave his watch to Capt. Tabb, to take outside the prison and sell for something to eat. Tabb, not accounting for the watch, after several days, the prisoner ventured to ask him where it was, when Tabb indignantly denied having it. The officer spoke of complaining to higher authority,— when Capt. Tabb seized, bucked and gagged, and otherwise

shamefully abused him. A day or two since he found a hole
dug in the ground where he suspected some one was digging a
tunnel by which to escape. He abused everybody for this, and
hammered Maj. Basco over the head with the butt of a musket
because he refused to fill the hole up, not having dug it.

These are only specimens of the indignities, insults and
abuses heaped upon us here almost daily.

The weather is very hot now. We have built some sheds,
that keep most of us out of the hot sun. Still, there are many
who remain out on the ground, in the sun and rain.

The prison we are now in is called "Camp Oglethorpe."

On the night of the 12th it rained very hard. I went
down near to the opening under the sink to see what prospect
there was for getting out there and escaping. I had not stood
there long when Capt. Gesner came down and stopped near the
spring by me. He had only been there a minute when the flash
of a gun blazed out of the darkness, and Gesner was dead. He
only gasped, "water, water." We asked an investigation of
the murder, but received no satisfaction. He was not on the
dead line when he was shot, but standing where he had a right
to.

During the last month we had been hard at work digging
a tunnel by which to make our escape. It was four feet under
the ground, and extended under the dead line and by the sentry-boxes, a distance of seventy-five feet. It was ready for use,
when some spy revealed it, and we were discovered—weeks of
labor thus being lost.

I am determined to escape from this prison hole, or lose
my life in the attempt.

Reports from Andersonville are horrible. Nearly all the

boys captured with me are already dead, and the hot weather
and starvation will soon take the remainder.

One of our sweetest comforts in this camp is the music
of the mocking birds, that occasionally fly into the tree tops,
over our camp, and sing for us hour after hour.

> "A light broke in upon my brain—
> It was the carol of a bird.
> It ceased, and then it came again—
> The sweetest song ear ever heard;
> And mine was thankful till my eyes
> Ran over with the glad surprise,
> And they that moment could not see
> I was the mate of misery.
> A lovely bird, with azure wings,
> And song that said a thousand things,
> And seemed to say them all for me !
> I never saw its like before,
> I ne'er shall see its likeness more.
> And it was come to love me, when
> None lived to love me so again,
> And cheering from my dungeon's brink
> Had brought me back to feel and think.
> I know not if it late were free,
> Or broke its cage to perch on mine,
> But knowing well captivity,
> Sweet bird ! I could not wish for thine."

CHAPTER V.

THE "rebs" are mourning sadly over the death of that old sinner—Lt. Gen. Polk. Sherman put a "quietus" on his treason, with a cannon-ball, the other morning, somewhere near Kennesaw Mountain. So they go. One by one they are dropping off, and going to answer for their wickedness.

The last rebel is in the army—the last dollar of the Treasury spent. "What's to be done, now!" say the alarmed leaders of the rebellion.

Grant is holding Richmond as though in a vice; while Sherman is rapping at the doors of Atlanta. It is not to be wondered at that the rebels tremble at the knees, and are growing desperate. It is a bitter cup they are drinking, but it is of their own choosing, and let them drain it to the dregs.

July 4th, 1864.—To-day many of us assembled in the hospital to celebrate the birth-day of the nation. We had speeches and songs for two hours. During the singing, an officer from Ohio drawing a miniature flag from his pocket, waved it above our heads. This created the wildest enthusiasm. Hats were waved and men cheered. It was the old flag in all its purity; and was it any wonder that tears ran down the checks of strong-hearted men?

Our noise brought in the commander of the camp, who ordered us to disperse at once, and not attempt to have a Yankee holiday in prison. "If we did not stop at once cannon would be opened on the prison." Of course we obeyed, though with the greatest reluctance.

To-day, July 15th, my term of enlistment expires. Three years a soldier, but I trust the time has not been spent in vain.

I have traded for a rebel uniform, and to-morrow I intend to try and make my escape under the guise of a rebel soldier. As the rebel Sergeants come in every morning at roll-call, I shall play Sergeant, and try to get out by the guards at the gate.

July 16th, and I am ready for an adventure. My suit of gray fits amazingly. Roll-call and the rebel Sergeants enter and the gate closes. With pencil and paper in hand I start. Over the dead line I go! The guards above the gate stare, but say nothing. I knock at the door of the stockade!

"What do you want?" says the Corporal, as he steps between me and the door.

"We are bothered about the rolls, Sir, and I am going out to see the officer of the guard!" and I passed by him, went around the prison, looked at the "Jonnies" eating breakfast, and then went up into the city of Macon.

A fine town, I preceived. Plenty of soldiers, plenty of darkies, and plenty of women, who look very sympathizingly upon the supposed "confed." soldier. But I must leave them all. So into the corn fields till night. Then the whole night is spent in wading through the dark swamps and listening to the hooting owls and croaking frogs. It is dark and dismal, but I am striking for freedom and my nerves seem strong. My old shoes are so worthless I can scarcely walk.

Daylight finds me in a blackberry-patch, where I remain all day Sunday. Ye gods! what a feast of berries for a hungry man.

All day I can hear the rebel trains of cars, as they rush up and down the railroad, to Atlanta. Oh, that I could be on a train, and moving rapidly away from prison.

The evening train stops near my hiding-place to wood and water. Now or never! Out I go, and slip into an empty freight-car. The whistle blows, and we are off for Atlanta—a hundred miles above.

It is moonlight, and I sit in the car, watching the farms, the houses, the towns,—and wandering what will turn up next.

At Lagrange we stop, again, and the conductor, in his rounds, finds me, alone in my glory.

"Who are you, sir?" he exclaims.

"A Confederate soldier, sir, of the Ninth Alabama Infantry—on my way to Atlanta, to join my regiment," I unhesitatingly answered.

"Let me have your fare, sir!"

"I am a Southern soldier—out of money—and cannot pay you; but I must ride to Atlanta. Beside, you dare not put a soldier off the train."

He grumbles a few words, and leaves me—again in my glory—to consider the "uncertainties of human events." Before daylight we are in Atlanta, and I feel much like a stranger in a strange place.

I enter a barn-yard that seems to be empty; up into

the hay-loft, to sleep until morning. Daylight comes, and
reveals the yard full of rebel cavalry—and a yankee in the
feed-mow! Horrible! What will I do? They will soon
come up for feed, and I am gone. Ah! here's an empty hogshead; into it I climb, and for six long hours, sit and lis-.
ten to the rebel tales of adventure. How they slew the "un-
godly yankees;" how they made "drinking-cups of his skull,"
and "money-bags of his scalp." Oh! terrible, terrible. My
knees, for once, do feel a little weak! But noon comes.—
They mount, and ride out; the terrible suspense ends, and I
emerge from the hogshead, and march out into the city—
with my bones inside my flesh, and my "scalp" still on my
head.

Nothing to eat, and no money; a pretty "fix," truly.
Here is the whole rebel army defending the city against
Gen. Sherman, who is making rapid strides in this direction. Surely he will succeed, and capture the city; then I
will be free. So I will hide in this empty house, for a day
or two, and something may "turn up."

Up I go, on the ceiling above, and listen to Sherman's
guns, that are now throwing shell into, and spreading conster-
nation throughout, the city.

Not half an hour has passed, ere a fugitive family—flying from the shot and shell in the lower part of the city—
come to the door, and remark: "It seems to be a safe place,
and we will move in." The carts are unloaded, and in they
come—wife, babies and all.

What a situation now; certainly something has "turned
up!" I have ears, and must hear the conversation that
transpires.

3

"Well, Mary, our army is whipped, and the city will be surrendered—wont it? Ah, dear!"

"Yes, Billy, but what of that! Are n't we just as good 'yankees' as them, then? And besides, I am dying for some *real* coffee, and sugar, and tea! Oh, yes; we'll be 'Union-folks,' then, and we'll live so nice—for I am tired of corn-coffee, and such like. And I tell you, we must make a 'yankee flag,' and raise it on the house-top, when Sherman comes, and then we'll claim protection as Union citizens, and draw rations for nothing—just like the rest of the Union-folks in the South. And here, Tom, is a 'hundred-dollar bill;' run and buy two yards of 'red calico!'—there's just enough money to pay for it! We'll manage 'em, won't we, though? Of course, we are rebels; but, you know, 'when you are among Romans, you must do as Romans do.'"

"It's a capital idea! Let the house burn! We'll be 'Union,' and the Yankee Government will pay us three times what it's worth."

"Yes, Tom, run and buy the flag; and as soon as the Yankees come I'll run to Sherman and apply for 'protection papers' and rations."

In an hour supper was ready, and the party went out under the awning to eat.

A slight inspection of the premises revealed but one way to get down, and that was by climbing down some pegs in the wall at the corner. But lo! a large bull dog is tied to the lower peg. What could I do? Nothing, without first making the acquaintance of the dog. I will try it! A lump of plaster on his nose causes him to look up in amazement. I smile on him. He smiles in return. He is a clever dog. I climb down the pegs, pat him on the head, slip out at the back door,

and go around the house to the awning in front, where the kind
'Union' people ask me to supper, which I, being 'Union,' too,
couldn't have the heart to refuse.

I ate heartily, put a lunch in my pocket, thanked the
'Union' family, left, and was then ready for "something to
turn up" again.

I now spent a week running around the army, seeing the
troops, the fortifications, the batteries and the city.

My regiment, the 9th Alabama, is in Cheatam's corps, but
I seldom visit it, finding less danger of being detected away
from it than with it.

I have posted myself as to its numbers, officers, companies,
&c., so that when questioned in other parts of the army in regard to my regiment, I pass muster amazingly.

With a pocket full of crackers and forged passes from Division commanders, I am enabled to inspect the army, its discipline, movements, &c., very much at my own leisure.

I have come across a loyal Irishman, by the name of——,
to whom I revealed myself, and who fed me in his cellar for
several days, when the rebel General Loring took up his headquarters in the yard, rendering it unsafe for me in the cellar.

On the 22d of July great preparations were making for a
grand charge on Sherman's left. I heard of it and determined
to attempt to get through the lines during the battle.

By 2 o'clock the bugles sounded, and the battle was soon
raging.

I followed in the rear of one of the Divisions, as an Ord-
nance Sergeant, thinking the rebel lines would be repulsed,
when I could lie down and remain on the ground until the
Federal lines came up. But at this point the rebels were vic-

torious, and I had the sorrow of seeing the "Boys in Blue," many of whom I recognized as from my own State, shot down, or brought back wounded and prisoners.

"General McPherson is killed!" shouted some one; and the whole line gave cheer upon cheer for the death of my old and loved Corps commander.

I could not get through the lines here, so with a heavy heart I started in an opposite direction, and by noon of the next day had made my way through two lines of infantry and one of cavalry, when I was arrested as a spy within five hundred yards of our own lines, on the Chattahoochie river.

I was in an obscure path in the woods, when a rebel vidette called a halt, and, as Shakspeare says, "stand and unfold."

"Surrender and hold up your arms!" cried a rebel in shoulder straps. "Who are you, and what are you doing down here in the woods by yourself?"

"Samuel Hawkins, Company B, Ninth Alabama," I replied. "I was out with a friend picking blackberries, and my horse, which was a borrowed one, broke loose and ran into the woods, and I am hunting him."

"Do you not know, sir, that you are almost into the jaws of yankees, who are not five hundred yards from here?".

"Indeed!" I exclaimed, with the greatest seeming amazement.

"Yes sir, you are, and the yankees have your horse before this time."

By this time half a dozen "Jonnies" had come to the spot from the rocks and brush around us.

" On right, on left, above, below—
Sprang up at once the lurking foe:
From shingles gray their lances start —
The bracken brush sends forth the dart.
The rushes and the willow wand
Are bristling into axe and brand,
And every tuft of brown gives life
To plaided warrior armed for strife."

And now suspicious glances and strange nods were exchanged between the armed fellows who looked on me as a
mountain bear.

"You are from Alabama," says one of them, " now tell me
where,—I am an Alabamian, too."

" Tullahoma, sir."

" Ah! I know nothing of that place," he replied.

" I cannot help that, sir, that's where I enlisted, and, for
that matter, where I was born."

" We must search you, sir, for it is my opinion that you
are a yankee *spy!* and one of the men here saw you in the city
on Sunday."

" Very likely he did, for I was in the city on business last
Sunday."

The search proceeded, but I had no papers about me only
a Bible under my shirt—(these pages were secreted in Macon)
—which was turned through and through, with the hope of
finding some hidden information as to who I was.

" Boys, take the prisoner to General Ross immediately,
and tell him I send him a man believed to be a yankee spy.—
Also hand the General these papers, giving particulars of his
arrest."

Things looked a little squally! Arrested as a spy, and

proof, too, that I had been lurking around the city and army; all of which was true.

Only a few moments previous and my heart was beating high with the hopes of home, and seeing the old Flag of Freedom again. Besides, I had information concerning the rebel army which I knew would be invaluable to General Sherman. But now how different! Once more a prisoner, in barbarous hands, and an alarming prospect of being hung as a spy!

Over rock, and hill, and hollow I marched, with a rebel cavalryman in front of me, and one behind, to prevent my attempting to escape.

Up among the rocks and trees, in a secluded spot, almost impracticable for horsemen to reach, was the headquarters of Brig. Gen. Ross, who received me as a prisoner, but treated me as a man. He ordered me something to eat and a blanket to rest upon.

At midnight I left this gentlemanly officer, and was taken to the Division commander, General Hume,—an old brute in appearance as well as actions. His only words to me were contemptible threats as to what he would do, should I dare to attempt an escape from him. He was sitting by a log fire, washing potatoes, and indulging in low slang about the yankees.

All night a rebel sat at my head with a revolver between his knees.

I did not sleep that night.

At daylight I was conducted to the headquarters of Gen. Hood, who commanded the rebel army.

On my way up I conversed with the guard, who seemed very communicative.

I easily persuaded him to show me the papers he was carrying up for my benefit. By these I had certain proof that I was considered a spy.

We found Hood, the one-legged general, quartered in tents in one of the door-yards of the city.

My letters of "introduction" were handed to a clerk, who, without looking at them, tossed them into a pigeon-hole, and directed me to the guard-house, where I remained until the next day.

All was excitement at headquarters. Lieutenants and orderlies were dashing everywhere at once.

The Provost Marshal of the army came to dispose of the visitors in the guard-house. One by one they were marched out and sent off somewhere. Col. Hill, Provost Marshal, seemed to be a perfect gentleman. Not one harsh word fell from his lips that morning, though some of the prisoners were hardened, desperate men, and deserters from the rebel army.—He approached me with a smile, and, not having received the papers, or information as to who I was, said:

"Your name, prisoner, if you please."

"I am a Federal prisoner, sir, who escaped from Macon, but was re-captured in the woods, yesterday."

"That indeed! Have you been about the city, or the fortifications, or the army, any?"

"Oh, no! I had just reached this vicinity when re-captured," I replied.

"Did you walk all of that hundred miles through the woods, my boy?"

"Certainly, I have no horses at my disposal."

"Well," said the Colonel, "I am most sorry you did not get through. You deserve a better fate than to be returned to prison; but I hope you may soon be exchanged. War is very bad, and prison is worse; but it is my duty, and I will send you back to prison at Macon."

An hour later and I was on the train bound for Macon, but thankful it was not the scaffold, and I rejoiced in the carelessness of that boyish clerk.

Should this ever meet the eyes of Col. Hill, of Nashville, he will smile, and be glad to know I lived through prison, for I know he is a man in whose breast the milk of human kindness flows warm and lasting, and that he will pardon the yarns I told him on that, to me, eventful occasion.

The next morning I was stripped of my rebel uniform, and with only my drawers and shirt turned into the pen from which I had escaped ten days before.

A fellow-officer furnished me with a pair of trowsers, and I now had ample time to reflect on what I had seen of the rebels, their fortifications and their way of fighting.

My observations convinced me of the superior discipline, at least in time of battle, of the rebel army over our own.— There was no choice—everything was compulsion. In battle they marched with a line of cavalry in rear of each command, to arrest and drive all stragglers into duty. Still, with all the force, and want of choice, the rebel privates fought with terrible desperation, and were extremely enthusiastic in their manifestations over the least sign of victory. They did not read as much as the private soldiers from the North, and consequently only knew of their own defeats when witnessed by themselves. No one dared to say anything to discourage the soldiers. Silence only saved those from punishment who were not intensely loyal to the Southern cause.

Everybody was in the army, save the few who possessed special claims on the friendship of the Richmond Rulers, and they were protected only by special exemption from the Secretary of War or Jeff. Davis himself. Even these were seized upon at times, and hurried to the battle front.

.. With their wholesale conscription of men any money, and their dreadful discipline in times of danger, they fought, and fought well.

They were materially aided by the positive, even desperate positions taken by the entire Southern press. For a newspaper to intimate surrender, or terms, was to invite destruction,—not by mob violence, but by the Rebel Government itself. The Southern press, used as it was, was a powerful engine to further the objects of the South.

How different the case in some parts of the North, where the press discouraged the people, advised mutiny, desertion, surrender, and everything that could retard the Government in its struggles for self-preservation.

Who can say the number of lives that might have been saved, or how much sooner the war might have been closed had the Government exercised its lawful authority in punishing the miserable, sneaking traitors, who sold themselves to crime and treason, that they might lick the feet of their Southern masters.

Who shall say how much of the sorrow of the whole land, North and South, can be laid at the doors of the cowardly rebels who control such journals as the Chicago *Times!*—men hated by the people of the section where they live, and despised even by those in the South for who's favors they have fawned ?

CHAPTER VI.

Shortly after my return to Macon, rumors came of another move to the South. Charleston was not only blockaded, but besieged.

Fort Sumpter was demolished, and the "Swamp Angel" chimed in the chorus from Morris Island, in tones that sent terror to many a rebel in the Palmetto city.

Slowly the city was melting away, under the continued shelling from the yankee batteries.

"It must be stopped!" cried the Charlestonians. "It shall be stopped!" came from Richmond.

"If we cannot prevent firing on the city with our own men, we will surprise the world by making 'breastworks of our prisoners.'"

A capital idea! and in perfect consonance with the rebel notions of civilized war.

Six hundred officers were selected—myself among the number—to be placed under the fire from our own guns.— Some weeks previous a number of the officers had organized a secret society, whose object should be to overpower the guards, the first favorable opportunity, and attempt an escape. The organization was complete, and unknown to even the prisoners who were not members. The penalty for violation of the orders from the Head Centre was instant death. Every member was in readiness to perform his part, in case an opportunity should offer. Most of the organization was chosen, unintentionally perhaps, to be taken to Charleston.

At a certain point on the route, (Pocatalico, South Carolina,) the train would pass within a few miles of the Federal gunboats, near the coast.

Then would be our time. We would make a desperate effort for freedom. When the train reached the proper point we would over-power our guards, take their arms, and fight our way to the coast. It was a practicable scheme, for there were but few rebels between Pocatalico and the coast. The guard on the train did not number over two hundred men, and there were six hundred of us prisoners. We could easily seize the guns from the guards inside the train, and then, by force of arms, compel the force on top of the cars to surrender.

Everything was in readiness. Most of us had short clubs tied up in our blankets, with which to fight, and everything seemed propitious. The night was dark, and the Fates seemed to smile on our undertaking.

We left the city of Savannah by dark, and by midnight would reach the point from which to strike. Our signal to strike was to be a red light, waved from the front car, by Capt. ——, of the Regular Army,—who was one of the leaders of the organization.

Midnight came; we were straining our eyes to see the red

light as we neared the place. Every heart beat high with excitement. Morning would find us free men, we thought, and
eagerly we watched; but no lights came. What was wrong?
Were we discovered? Bitter, bitter thought!

. We whirled by the village at which the blow was to be
given; the train did not stop—no light appeared—and in an
hour we were in the city of Charleston; not free, but prisoners still,—and worse than all, victims of the cowardice of one
man, and he our leader.

· When the train reached the proper point this "gallant
Captain," who had solemnly sworn to stand by us, allowed his
heart to fail him, and thus stamped himself an infamous coward.

The Charleston papers learned of the intended movement
to escape, by the prisoners, and in commenting upon the pro-
posed arrangements, admitted them to have been most complete, and declared that nothing but incompetency on the part
of some of our leaders prevented an escape of the entire
number.

We were marched to the city jail, and confined in the
yard,—surrounded by a brick wall, a portion of which was
built by the British, for prisoners, during the Revolutionary
war.

We were hungry, tired, and nothing short of "maddened."
Many and severe were the imprecations pronounced on the
head of him who had deserted, when Liberty was within our
grasp.

"Lynch him!" strongly urged some of the more desperate, and his removal to a safer point, by the rebels whom he
had served too well, saved him, perhaps, from his just
deserts. ~

The city jail was the best I had ever seen; but the yard, in which we were placed, was filthly and hot.

We found Charleston to be a fine city, of one hundred thousand inhabitants. The private residences are very fine; the streets are good, and nicely shaded by the finest trees of the South. Many of the gardens contain the orange, lemon, magnolia and holly trees. In times of peace this· was one of the most flourishing cities of the South.

We were suffering greatly in the jail yard, when the commanding officer told us if we would give our parole not to attempt an escape, they would put us in better quarters, and furnish more rations. Of course we signed the parole, which was to be valid only while we remained in Charleston. We were now placed in a large building—near the burned district —known as the "Roper Hospital." We had plenty of room, here, and a large, pleasant yard to walk in; but the yard was our limits, as the guards were posted around on the outside of the fence.

We are still under fire from our guns, on Morris Island, and an occasional shot, from the "Swamp Angel," comes howling into the city; but thus far none of us have been hurt, as the shots are of a high range, and pass harmlessly over our heads—crashing into the city beyond.

From our south window we have a fine view of the Ashly river. Between us and the river, and far away to the left, is seen that portion of the city known as the "burned district." It is a great, black field of desolation,—nothing being left but ruined towers, toppling chimneys, and piles of brick and mortar. The streets are overgrown with weeds and grass.— No one lives there, and but few visit the place, save the little boys and girls—who go to the deserted grounds to gather figs and grapes, to sell on the streets.

Never before have I seen such dark and sorrowful desolation as this picture presents. It reminds us of the fearful judgment, pronounced against a certain people by the Prophet Isaiah—

"And thorns shall come up in her palaces—nettles and brambles in the fortresses thereof; and it shall be an habitation of dragons, and a court for owls. The screech-owl shall rest there, and find for herself a place of rest. There shall the great owl make her nest and lay, and hatch, and gather under her shadow. There shall the vultures also be gathered, every one with his mate."

Maj. Gen. Johnson, and Brig. Gen. Jeff. Thompson—known as the "Swamp Fox"—visited the prisoners to-day.—They have just been exchanged, and spoke very freely of the *kind treatment* they received, while prisoners in the North. Jeff. is a keen-looking "fox," is a good runner, and has served the Confederacy many a good turn by his cowardly, guerrilla warfare. The rebels should confer some title on him. I would suggest "Knight of the Swamp."

To-day we sent North for some gold which we can exchange for Confederate money at the rate of one dollar in gold for five in rebel notes—of which it requires thirty-six dollars to buy a bushel of potatoes; so that very desirable vegetable costs us over five dollars in gold to the bushel.

Weather continues very warm, but we have a sea breeze most of the time, which renders the heated days of August bearable.

This is nearly the last of August, and I have not a word from home since last March.

The rebels appear to be in very excellent spirits just now,

and profess to think General Grant a failure; still, few of them expect peace this year.

All day yesterday, and most of the night, the city was shelled from the batteries on Morris Island. Many of the shells passed near the building in which we are quartered. Some of the shells now thrown into the city, are thrown from batteries five miles away. Many of them pass by the building and some fall in the yard; but as yet no one has been injured by them. They are a greater source of alarm to the rebel guards than they are to the prisoners. It is amusing to the prisoners to see how frequently the guards will drop flat on their faces when a shell comes in close proximity to the building.

Sunday night the rebels burned the town of Legareville, a few miles below the city, to prevent its being used by the Federals.

. The rebel press of the Confederacy are bolstering up the spirits of the Southern people, by telling them that the peace men of the North will soon compel the Federal Government to suspend hostilities, and thus secure independence to the South.

Great hopes are entertained by the rebels that the Democratic Convention, which meets in Chicago, will nominate a peace candidate for the Presidency.

The weather continues very sultry, even for this hot climate.

We have good news now from Mobile, Alabama. Three of the largest forts guarding the city are now in our hands, namely: Morgan, Powell and Gaines, captured with several rebel gunboats by Admiral Farragut.

The shells are still coming into the city at a terrible rate. From the window where I write I can see the monster

200 pound Parrots explode every few minutes, yet it is a magnificent spectacle to watch them sailing almost among the stars, then darting down to explode in the streets of the city.

Yesterday evening there was a heavy rain-storm, accompanied by wind, lightning and thunder. Two or three houses were struck by lightning.

This morning, (August 25th,) we have good news from Gen. Grant. The enemy attacked him last Sunday, and drove him from the Weldon road, and were repulsed with great slaughter. Of course this was received by us with great joy.

We are now receiving the best rations we have had issued to us in the Confederacy. We have flour, corn-meal, rice and fresh beef.

Another severe storm of wind and rain raged this afternoon, which caused great commotion on the bosom of the old Ashly river, together with an extensive tumbling of old chimneys and towers in the burned district of the city.— But few shells were thrown by our batteries, during the storm. One of those thrown passed into the quarters of some of the prisoners; but luckily did no harm, save spoiling some rations.

The rebels are boasting to us, to-day, that they have won great victories in Virginia, capturing many guns, prisoners, etc.

The rebels are in very high spirits over the prospects of a "muss" in the North—to be raised by the copperheads, in Convention at Chicago. They claim that none but a "Peace-Candidate" will be nominated; and if nominated, of course will be elected, thus creating great dissatisfaction and trouble throughout the North.

August 31st.—The last day of Summer—going, going, gone. I spend my time reading such books as are to be had in prison; of course they are not always of my own choice, but to-day I have read a book entitled "*Lamb's Stories from Shakspeare.*" The book is neatly written, and a fine introduction to that great man.

The morning is cool, with a delightful sea-breeze blowing. No news from home, yet! How tired of waiting! Some of us are beginning to think the Government is neglecting its soldiers in the rebel prisons. Sometimes it really seems so. Still, we hope and pray our friends in the North have not forgotten us.

We now have some hopes of being removed from under our own fire, as six hundred rebel officers have been sent from the North, to join Géneral Foster on Morris Island, to be placed under fire, in retaliation for similar treatment to us in Charleston; but the probabilities are that they will soon be exchanged for an equal number of Federals, and each one of us hopes to be the lucky one.

We have news of heavy fighting at Atlanta, but the rebels refuse to give us the particulars.

A great fire occurred in the city last night, and while it was burning the shells came thick and fast from the Federal batteries on Morris Island. Three pieces of shell fell in our yard, but did no harm. We prisoners spent most of the night at the windows, watching the shells as they came thundering into the city.

News has been received of the nomination, at Chicago, of McClellan and Pendleton, on the peace platform. The rebels are in high glee over this bit of news.

A flag of truce boat came up the harbor, yesterday, by

4

which we learned that our prospects of exchange are very dull, and that "red tape" at Washington will prevent us receiving any money.

The rebels have at last admitted a victory for Gen. Sherman. He captured Atlanta. This will be an agreeable offset to the Peace resolutions at Chicago.

The correspondence relative to an exchange of prisoners is published to-day. The rebels made propositions to exchange on the 10th of August, which have not been replied to at this date. It seems as if Secretary Stanton desires no exchange at all, or else he is outrageously slow in his efforts! The day is turning out beautiful after last night's storm. We have little that is definite, from Atlanta; only that the rebel, Gen. Hood, the one-legged man, was soundly threshed out of the city, and hotly pursued.

The notorious rebel, Gen. Morgan, who alarmed the North to such a degree by his raids into Ohio, has been killed in East Tennessee, to which we say—amen.

There is a sort of a museum connected with the hospital, here, to which is attached a dissecting-room. To-day a friendly rebel invited me to go in with him, and see the sights; I went, when he showed me a leg amputated from the first soldier killed in the present war. He was a Federal, and was killed in April, 1861, at Fort Sumpter. A piece of the shell which produced the fatal wound, is still to be seen in the limb. This has been preserved in liquor, by the rebels, as a curiosity for the chivalry.

Two of the rebel pirates have been captured lately, the Alabama and the Georgia.

The Charleston papers now consider their prospects of independence darkened, by their recent reverses in Georgia and Alabama.

This week seven thousand prisoners have been brought to Charleston. They are all privates, and are quartered in the Race Course, having no protection whatever from the sun and storm.

Firing on the city is still kept up by the Federal batteries, killing a man occasionally.

Arrangements have been made to exchange Naval officers; but the prospects of Army officers going home, soon, are slender.

The weather is delightful; the cool sea-breeze is blowing almost constantly. Yesterday there was a large fire in the vicinity of the prison: all the fire-companies—black, white and yellow—were out and labored till dark with the fire, and all the night with whisky. Gen. Foster cannonaded the city at a terrible rate, while the fire lasted, and as the shells were thrown at the firemen, many of them came in close proximity to the prison. One shell struck the building, passed through the rooms, and slightly injured one prisoner. Many pieces of shell fell in the yard.

During the conflagration the white and black firemen,—who were pumping in front of the prison, drank whisky, from the same bottle, and got "gloriously drunk," together. What a people to talk of abolitionism, and sneer at negro equality.

It is now the middle of September. Cases of Yellow Fever were brought into the city, by blockade-runners, and the epidemic is raging among all classes of people. Of course the alarm among the prisoners is very great,—knowing as we do that should the disease break out in the prison, there will be but little hope for escape from death.

We had sweet potatoes for breakfast, this morning, and corn-cakes for dinner. . Potatoes are $36,00 per bushel. Gold is worth $28,00 for $1,00, Confederate, on the streets; but rebel sharpers compel us to give one dollar in gold in exchange for five dollars in Confederate currency. Many of us submit to this swindle as the rations have grown beautifully less!

Gen. B. F. Butler, agent for exchange, has written a letter to the New-York *Times*, which, if adhered to by the Government, will prevent an exchange of prisoners during the war. The point on which the two governments contend seems to be the negro soldier; and we fear the difficulty will remain long unsettled.

The morning papers contain reports of Gen. Early having received a severe castigation, at the hands of the gallant Phil. Sheridan. The rebels admit their loss in killed and wounded to be terrible. This is the expedition that was to threaten (!) Washington, and 'carry "fire and sword" into Pennsylvania.

Later papers give us the particulars of the battle, which was, indeed, desperate,—and resulted in a complete victory to the National arms; yet many, many brave sons of freedom have fallen, and even the glad cheers of victory will be mingled with the groans for our noble slain.

AFTER THE BATTLE.

After the battle; and loud the gun
Belches the tale of a battle won.
A battle won, and the vict'ry ours —
Strew the laurel, and twine the flowers.

After the battle; 'tis twice we've won
These bays, and laurels we now put on.
Twice we have filled these new-made graves—
Rather than live like cringing slaves.

After the battle; but who shall know
How many, and bitter, the tears that flow?
How many—how sad the hearts—that wail
The deadly path of the iron hail.

After the battle; and this is all—
Save the farewell gun, and the plumeless pall.
They bear our dead to the silent shore—
Silent and lone—Ah! evermore.

Generals Sherman and Hood have agreed upon a special exchange of one hundred and thirty officers, captured this Summer. My messmate, Lieut. Sill, hopes to be among the number; if so I will take the opportunity of sending a letter to my friends, in the North, in answer to one I received this morning, which tells me "all are alive and well." It is the most welcome letter I have ever received,—enabling me to rest easier, as my anxiety is less.

Last night the city was again furiously shelled—many of the bombs bursting fearfully close to our prison quarters.

There are now one thousand rebel officers on Morris Island, in retaliation for our condition. Remarkable times, indeed—when prisoners of war are used as targets!

Jeff. Davis is up to Macon, Georgia, making speeches—in which he says: "Sherman shall soon be driven out of the city with great disaster."

The rebel, Gen. Early, has again been whipped by "little Phil." Poor Early! he had better go back to his guardian—

"Bobby Lee." He has lost all his cannons and about half of his men.

Last night the city was more severely bombarded than at any time during the siege. The shells averaged one in every two minutes.

The yellow fever is still raging in the city. Many rebels, who guarded us, have fallen victims to the epidemic. Last night the captain in command of the prison, and his adjutant, died, and were hauled out this morning.

The men who are at the Race Course are suffering greatly. No shelter and but little food. We hear of their conditions through the Sisters of Charity—Catholic ladies, who spend most of their time in trying to do good, and to alleviate the sufferings of all in the city—both friend and foe. They tell us the boys at the Race Course are being swept off by starvation, exposure, and the frightful ravages of the yellow fever. We are now told that out of fifty of our fellow-officers, who were victims of the disease, and taken out of this prison, but one is alive.

CHAPTER VII.

THE rebels, on the 5th inst., placed all of the officers, who were prisoners, on board the cars, and ran us down to Columbia, South Carolina—the Capital of the State. Numbers escaped on the route, but were mostly re-captured.— Some were killed in the attempt to escape.

Columbia is probably the handsomest town in South Carolina, besides being the Capital. On our arrival at the city we were turned out into an open lot, and remained there during a terrible rain-storm. At this place Lt. Clark was bayonetted, by the guard, for attempting to buy a loaf of bread of another guard.

After remaining in these "quarters" one day we were removed to within two miles of the city, near the Congaree river—a wide and rapid stream, but not navigable.

Maj. Marshall, Captains Page and Bascom, and Lieut. Hoffman, of my regiment, with many others, have escaped from the cars. They are persevering men, and I think they will make their way to the North. God grant that they may, for they have endured much in prison, and more than deserve their freedom. *

We have called our new prison "Camp Sorghum," from the fact that we receive little for rations, here, but "sorghum molasses" and corn-meal—the molasses not half boiled and almost green in color. The field in which we are placed is entirely open, but surrounded by a forest of pine trees,—which we can only look at, wishing ourselves free and happy as the birds among their branches. We have no tents for shelter, but build houses of pine boughs,—which keep off the sun, but are no protection from the rain.

The nights are quite cool; we have but few blankets, consequently all of us suffer. We have had no meat issued to us, and but little wood for fires.

The majority of the officers who escaped from the train, between here and Charleston, were chased down by bloodhounds and captured,—and this, too in the chivalrous State of South Carolina. Our band at this time numbered 1500.

Yesterday our hearts were made glad by the receipt of a few boxes of clothing, and other articles, sent us from the North. My share was one flannel shirt and one towel.

In view of the approaching election in the North, and the great interest taken in it by the people, we concluded to have an election of our own. Accordingly, notices were posted up through the camp, that all who wished to vote for President could do so, at a certain officer's quarters in the pris-

* I have learned that these officers, after several nights of fatiguing march, and many narrow escapes, succeeded in reaching the Federal lines in East Tennessee.

on. Every man cast a vote, and the result was as follows:

For Lincoln...1,024
For McClellan... 143

This was the voice of men who had endured hardships, suffering and starvation, but could not nor would not give their votes for a degrading peace.

Many officers attempt to escape at night by running over the dead-line and passing the guards during the darkness. Of course, many are crippled, and some lives lost, by these attempts. The dead-line is only an imaginary line, marked by an occasional stick, twelve feet inside the outer guard line.— Any one seen approaching this line is instantly shot.

I have traded for a suit of Confederate clothes, forged some passes, and intend to attempt my escape on the first dark night.

Last night I sat up the greater part of the night, watching for an opportunity, but the moon shone brightly, and I dared not attempt to run the line.

Lieutenant Young, of the Fourth Pennsylvania Cavalry, while quietly sitting by his fire, yesterday evening, conversing with friends, was shot dead by one of the guards. Of course we all ran to the spot to see who was killed, when the rebel in command ordered us to disperse immediately or he would open the artillery on the camp.

The officer commanding the artillery posted near the camp has orders to open upon us the moment five shots have been fired by the guard.

Scarcely a night passes by but some one attempts to escape, and the guards fire. Of course there is no telling when the fatal five shots may be fired, and the entire camp swept to destruction.

Captain Dirks attempted to run over the dead-line, but received a shot in the leg.

We have no tents, and are drawing miserably poor rations. For many days our only rations have consisted of corn meal, and molasses of the worst sort.

The nights are chilly and cold, and often accompanied by severe rains. We have not sufficient fuel, and of course our sufferings are great. The little wood we receive, wo carry on our backs nearly a quarter of a mile.

On the 4th of November, while out with the others after wood, I determined to again attempt my escape. Quietly secreting myself in the brush, and not being missed by the guards who accompanied us, I remained there until night, when I started in a Westerly direction, in company with Lieutenant Fritchie, of St. Louis, who, also, had eluded the guards, and traveled nearly all night over sandy roads and through pine forests. The night was cold, dark and windy. By midnight we heard the hounds after us, but managed to elude them, and secreted ourselves in a corn crib, and slept soundly until 7 o'clock in the morning, when we again took to the woods and traveled most of the day.

Some other officers had escaped from prison, and the whole country was consequently on the watch for us. In the afternoon, leaving Lieutenant Fritchie in the bushes, I went into a house and purchased some corn bread. We then slept for two hours in the bushes, and at sundown started for a night's march. It was a desolate country—sandy bottoms and dark pine trees.

We had not proceeded far when we were met by two mounted rebels who were in the woods hunting deserters

from their own army. We were at once arrested, and started
on a march for Lexington Jail.

The officer who had charge of me spoke very kindly,
and gave me assurances that his sympathies were with the
North, but that he was suspected by the rebels, and dare not
aid me in the least. I tugged along by his side, talking
till midnight about the war and the South and its prospects
of success.

On arriving at Lexington, we were placed in one of the
cells, without blankets or food. We had remained there but
two hours when a little boy came to the prison door and
handed the jailor a basket and a blanket, saying that the
wife of the officer who had brought Lieutenant Byers there
sent them with her compliments. On removing the cover
from the basket, we found it well filled with warm biscuit and
other niceties which a person less hungry than I could well
appreciate.

WOMAN.

Even in the darkest hour of earthly ill,
Untarnished yet, thy fond affection glows,
Throbs with each pulse and beats with every thrill,
Bright o'er the wasted scene thou hoverest still.

Angel of comfort to the failing soul;
Undaunted by the tempest, wild and chill,
That pours its restless and disastrous roll
O'er all that blooms below, with and and hollow howl.

When sorrow rends the heart—when feverish pain
Wrings the hot drops of anguish from the brow,
To soothe the soul—to cool the burning brow,
O, who so welcome, and so prompt as thou!

Kind, sympathizing woman! Oh, how our hearts went

out to you! Prisoners, and strangers in a strange land, yet we were not forgotten.

The next day was Sunday. We spent it in jail with several other officers who had been captured. In the cell adjoining us was a woman confined for murder.

Lexington is a small country town, and its citizens had never beheld one of the "Lincoln hirelings, or horned yankees." Of course we were great objects of curiosity during the day.

All the impudent boys, and bashful maidens, and the talkative old ladies flocked to the jail to see the caged beasts. One very credulous young Miss expressed her surprise on discovering that the yankees had no "horns," as she had often been assured.

Our jailor is a crippled old rebel, who, judging from his language, has seen enough, as he expressed it, of "the cussed war."

On the following morning, a company of rebel home-guards, armed with bowie-knives and shot-guns, came to the jail to march us back to the Columbia prison. The day was very warm, and we were compelled to march most of the way without halting to rest. One of the officers complained of the forced march, stated that his feet had given out and that he could go no further, when one of the guard presented his shot-gun to his breast and, with an oath, ordered him to go on. The officer hobbled along as best he could, and at 3 o'clock we were again in prison.

All that we had accomplished by our adventure was a break in the monotony of prison life. We had some sport, and above all, had plenty of bread and bacon from the darkies, to whom we never feared confiding our secrets.

I would here testify to the universal loyalty of the colored people throughout the South. Several times have I been aided by them, while a prisoner, in my attempts to escape; and the testimony of scores of other officers, who have been assisted to escape by them, corroborates my statement. Nothing that they possessed was too good or too dear to be given to the white soldiers who were fighting to save the life of the nation, and whom they knew to be their friends. I have seen them go hungry and barefooted themselves, and travel all night as guides, giving their shoes to the escaped prisoners, and returning to their master's plantation with a certainty of receiving the severest punishment for their devotion to our cause.

At last we have heard the result of the Northern election, and are all rejoicing to know that it has resulted in an overwhelming victory to the Union party. Lincoln and Johnson have been the choice of the loyal North, as well as of the Union people of the South. The rebels are feeling very sore over the result, but cannot help it and so say little about it.

Our rations at the present consist of but a little sorghum and corn meal, with the smallest quantity of rice, so we are living very poorly.

Several thousand of the sick and wounded prisoners have been sent to Savannah to be exchanged, but no commissioned officers are among the number as yet.

I am messing at the present time with Lieut. Morris, a gallant young officer from Rock Island, Illinois, who has suffered, uncomplainingly, for many, many weary months.

Our quarters are a sort of cave dug in the ground— three feet by eight, and three feet deep—over which we placed pine boughs, covering them with dirt. It is more like a grave than a house,—having just room sufficient to lie side by side and sleep. In the lower end we have a small fire-place, in which we burn pine knots—affording us a little fire to cook by, and a light at night.

For several nights Lieut. Morris and myself have sat up the greater part of the night, in this little dungeon, reading old papers, talking over the past and wondering about the future.

All the boxes and provisions which have been sent us, by our friends in the North, with a very few exceptions, have been stolen by the rebels.

We are almost out of clothing. Many officers are going barefooted and bareheaded. To-day I am going in my drawers, in order that I may wash my only pair of pants.— Many of the officers have but a single shirt, and necessarily go half naked when washing it.

November 25th, 1864.—Camp Sorghum, South Carolina. To-day makes one year for me in prison—a long, dark, lonesome blank it has been in my existence. One year further on in life's journey, and nothing whatever has been accomplished. How much longer must this thankless suffering last. None but the two Governments can answer, and they will not.— Still, I am for my country, now and forever!

Lieut. Morris and myself have received an axe, and are now building a log cabin—hoping to live more comfortably.

We have news that Sherman has burned Atlanta, and has started on a campaign to the sea. Many prisoners escape from camp, and try to reach his lines; but are generally re-captured by the blood-hounds.

Last night my friend, Lieut. Ecking, of New-Jersey, was shot dead while attempting to pass the camp guard. In the evening he had offered the guard a watch if he would permit two or three to pass him during the night. He stepped over the dead-line, and going up to the guard presented him a watch, when he was instantly shot. He was a noble young man, and died in striking for liberty. Other officers have been shot, lately, but none killed.

The weather is rather warm, to-day. We have but little news from Sherman, as we are not allowed to see the papers.

Our only way of securing fuel is by giving our parole not to attempt an escape, when squads of three or four are allowed to pass the line into the woods, and bring what wood they can obtain without axes. Of course, by so slow a process only half the fuel necessary can be procured.

No meat has been issued to us for months. To-day a wild hog dashed out of the woods, passed the guards, and fearlessly crossing the dead-line, marched down through the camp. All hands were after the pork. Clubs, stones and axes were brought into requisition, and finally, having raced from one end of the camp to the other, "porkey" was compelled to "surrender;" he was brought down and divided into about one hundred rations. In a few minutes the rebel officers came in to see the cause of the alarm, when their attention was called to the hog's hide, and were told that we were no longer "Jews," but that that said "grunter" was "done gone!"

A man from Pocatalico came here with a pack of bloodhounds, to make his living by running down escaped prisoners. Every morning, at daylight, the hounds are raced around the outside of the camp, to see if any prisoner has escaped during the night; if any one has succeeded in evading the vigilance of the guards the hounds are at once put upon his track, and generally before night the unfortunate striker for liberty is returned to prison.

This morning two hounds, belonging to this pack, ventured into the camp among the prisoners. We immediately adopted a resolution that "these blood-hounds had caught their last yankee; and seizing the axe we cut their heads off, and threw them into an old well. The owner of the hounds, accompanied by an officer of the guard, immediately came in on the search. The lifeless bodies of the hounds were taken out from the well, with many a dire imprecation upon the heads of the yankee murderers. Threats were made that ere a week's time had passed two officers should pay the penalty with their lives. As it would seem, to carry out their hellish design, an officer who subsequently escaped, was caught in a tree by a rebel before the hounds reached the spot, and was ordered to come down from the tree; the hounds were called and set upon him—tearing him so fearfully that he died in a few days.

Most of our sleep is secured during the daytime, as it is too cold too sleep through the night. We spend the night in walking about, and when the sun rises we lie down to sleep.—Of course such unnatural habits are productive of unhealthful physical conditions, and many a victim is taken to the little grave yard, just opposite the camp.

The prison is now commanded by Maj. Griswold and Lt. Cooper—both South Carolinians.

Another officer, Lieut. Turbayne, of the Sixteenth New-York, was foully murdered, this morning, by one of the guards. He was walking along the path, near the dead-line, which path was often frequented by the prisoners, when the guard, a Mr. Williams, of Newbury Court House, presented his gun and ordered him to go back; the lieutenant immediately turned and walked back a step or two, when this hell-commissioned scoundrel shot him in the back—killing him instantly. This dastardly coward had often sworn that he would kill a yankee before he left the camp. We complained of the murderer to Maj. Griswold, in command, and demanded an investigation; but received no reply whatever. We had made threats that should this murderer ever be allowed in camp again, we would kill him. The next morning Maj. Griswold marched him into the camp—surrounded by a body guard—for the purpose of intimidating and humiliating the prisoners; as, of course, we dared not carry out our threats.

Yesterday one of the rebel guards was placed in the stocks for misconduct, when the whole rebel company refused to do duty. Troops were called out, and the entire company was arrested and sent to jail.

Our little cabins are now completed, and a majority of us have shelter; but no sooner are they completed than we have orders to prepare to go to another camp,—where we have to remain without shelter, again, for weeks or months.

December 12th.—To-day we were marched up into the city and placed in the enclosure belonging to the lunatic assylum. It is a small lot—one acre in extent—surrounded by a brick wall, twelve feet high. We have no shelter whatever, and the weather is very disagreeable; are allowed no papers, and can only guess at the events going on outside.

I have made an arrangement with a friendly negro to bring me an occasional rebel paper. I learn by one of them that Gen. Sherman has captured Savannah, and presented it to the President as a Christmas gift. Also that Gen. Thomas has whipped Hood's army twice, during the last month, in the vicinity of Nashville. Hood had fifteen generals killed and wounded. The fighting Irishman—Pat. Cleburne

—is among the killed. Hood has lost 5,000 men and 49 cannon in his last fight.

Defeat is now attending the rebels everywhere. So we prisoners can rejoice even amid our sorrows.

We do little in the camp but eat and sleep, as it is too cold for study. I walk about the camp the greater part of the nights.

Yesterday I composed the song entitled Sherman's March to the Sea. An officer—Lieut. Rockwell, of New York—has written music for it, and our Glee Club will soon sing it for the prisoners.

Savannah surrendered on Wednesday morning. So Sherman has completed the grandest campaign in history.

The rebels mourn considerably, and think that South Carolina will soon run red with blood. God grant that she may soon receive the just deserts of her crimes.

December 25, 1865.—This is my second Christmas in prison. The day is cold, dark and disagreeable. We have but little wood and can scarcely keep from freezing. We spent the day singing songs, dancing, hallooing, and running about the camp to keep from freezing.

I have received a little Confederate money, and Lieutenant Austin, my present messmate, and myself have added something to our bill of fare. For breakfast we had mutton soup and corn cakes.

The health of the prison is now pretty good—there being but 34 prisoners in the hospital.

I managed to get a few letters North a few days ago. Lt. Tower, of Ottumwa, Iowa, who had lost a leg in the army, and was afterwards captured, was now to be exchanged and sent home. He wears a hollow artificial limb in the place of the

one lost. This we packed full of letters, one of which contained
Sherman's March to the Sea. The rebels little suspected
our novel way of communicating with our friends. The Lieutenant went safely through, and the letters were all delivered.

Now that we have some barracks completed, we are enabled to have a little fire and light at night. At least one-half
the night is spent in playing cards, chess, &c.

Another new year is upon us, the war is not ended and we
are still in prison. Our greatest source of amusement is the
Glee Club and a string band organized in the prison. The
Glee Club consists of Major Isett, of Iowa, Captain Patterson,
of Washington City and Captain Daniels, of Massachusetts—
all good singers, who do much to drive away the dull hours of
prison life. The instruments were purchased by contribution
from the officers in Charleston. Lieutenant Rockwell plays
the flute, the two Captains Chandler accompany with the violin and bass viol.

The rebels often come in and call for music, and, strange
to say, will sometimes allow us to sing our national songs.—
Among others, Sherman's March to the Sea has been sung
and received with great applause,—the rebels themselves
encoring it.

This evening, when the Glee-Club was singing in front of
the Hospital, a rebel who had formerly belonged to our regular army, on hearing the "Star Spangled Banner" sung, said,
with tears in his eyes: " Boys, I am a rebel, but still I love to
hear your "Star Spangled Banner" sung, and to look on the
starry flag !

The weather now-a-days is very disagreeable. The wind
blows cold, and, with but little fire, the Christmas times are
anything but merry.

Occasional papers are received in camp which contain accounts of fighting at different points in the Confederacy, at all of which the rebels are being sadly defeated. This is the only consolation we have. So long as our armies are victorious we can bear imprisonment cheerfully.

Last night I played chess until midnight, when, half frozen, I went to bed and dreamed of happiness and home, but awoke this morning to find the reality a very different thing.

I washed my clothes to-day, and think I did a very nice job of it. I am also an expert hand at baking pancakes.

We have received more Confederate money, which is worth about three cents on the dollar. Still, my mess lives a little better than heretofore.

Beef is now selling at $4 per pound. Potatoes $25 per bushel. Butter $14 per pound. Star candles $24 per pound. Lard $14 per pound. Flour $500 per bbl.

The above prices I copied from this morning's *South Carolinian*. What little meat my mess eats now costs $8 per day, as the rebels have not issued a bit of meat for months. They have never issued a stitch of clothing, and some of the officers here in camp are entirely barefooted and bareheaded.

We have news that Sherman has left Savannah, and is marching into South Carolina.

The city of Savannah has returned to the Union, and claims protection from the Government. She has acted wisely, and the indications are that other cities, and even States, may do likewise.

Troops are daily passing through the city to confront Sherman. They are mostly South Carolinians, fighting on their own soil. They appear to be in high spirits, as they cheer vociferously when passing the prison.

Frank Blair has arrived in Richmond on a peace mission. What will come of it, no one knows, and we prisoners care less; but would prefer to see him remain at home, and the war prosecuted until traitors are willing to lay down their arms and return to their allegiance. Powder and lead are the only agents that will bring about a permanent peace with rebels. Every man in prison is opposed to making them any concessions whatever. The only privileges we would give them would be the benefit of the Confiscation Act and the payment of the war debt, after enforcing the Emancipation Proclamation to the letter. They are rebels, and not revolutionists; and as such should be punished to the extent of the law. If the cup be bitter, it is of their own choosing. Let them drain it to the dregs.

On the 19th inst. we received news of the capture of Fort Fisher, on Cape Fear River, near Wilmington. The rebel General Whiting was captured with the garrison. This fort was the key to Wilmington, and of course the city will soon be in our hands.

For some strange reason Butler failed to capture the forts, and returned North.

The rebels are now becoming desperate, and demand that the slaves be armed at once. Six months ago they declared that to arm the slaves was to abandon the whole principle of the contest; for of course emancipation must be granted the slave as a reward for his services. "Oh, consistency, thou art a jewel!"

Senator Foote, of the rebel Congress, has been arrested as an enemy to the South, and so the ball rolls on.

The Peace-Commission, composed of Stevens, of Georgia, Hunter, of Virginia, and Campbell, of Alabama, met President Lincoln at Fortress Monroe, who informed them that a peace could only be attained by the rebels laying down their arms and returning to their allegiance.

The Congress of the United States has amended the Constitution so as to prohibit slavery forever. The prisoners rejoice at this, and thank God for it.

I have learned that my former messmate, Major Ed. E. Sill, of Livonia, N. Y., who escaped with two or three others from Camp Sorghum, has reached the North in safety. They spent many nights in climbing over the mountains of Tennessee, through deep snow and cold storms of winter. Major Sill traveled the last two nights of his terrible journey barefooted, having lost his shoes while wading a rapid stream in the mountains. He bore his prison life with a brave heart, and now, by persevering through toil and danger, he is at home, breathing the free air of the old Empire State.

General Sherman's army is now at Branchville, and the authorities of this city are very much frightened lest he shall march here and release the prisoners, and, perhaps, burn the city, as it deserves.

They now begin to talk of moving us to some point of safety, but to what particular locality no one knows, as the safe points in the Confederacy are few and far between.

I have concluded that should they move us again to make another desperate attempt to escape.

The rebel General Winder, the inhuman commander of all the prisons in the South, died on the 11th inst. He dropped dead from a stroke of paralysis. On the announcement of his death the prisoners greatly rejoiced, and some of them raised a mud monument in the center of the camp, on which was inscribed the last words of the tyrannical general: " Cut off the molasses, boys." Another inscription was: "General Winder died and went to Hell. The Devil, thinking himself superceded, turned out the guard to receive him."

Winder was the most inhuman brute, perhaps, in the whole Confedemcy, and, next to Davis, the most powerful. It was by his orders that all the suffering and starvation at Andersonville, and other prisons in the South, was brought about.

On the 13th of February we received orders to be ready to move at a moment's notice. I resolved to remain behind as long as possible, and for the third time try to effect an escape. The weather was cold and disagreeable. On the 14th 600 officers were placed in cattle cars and hurried away from the city.

The reports now were that Sherman, with a large army, was marching on the city. On the night of the 15th tho remainder of the officers were taken out of the camp and marched to the depot, and started for North Carolina.

Lieutenant Devine, of Philadelphia, and myself have arranged a plan for escape. We have removed a board from the ceiling in the hospital, making an opening through which we may pass into the garret above, and perhaps elude the guard till the troops are marched away.

The prisoners were taken away this morning at daylight, and Lieutenant Devine and myself remained in our hiding places listening to tho rebels below hunting for us. All day they searched—under the barracks, in holes in the ground, and in every conceivable place that they imagined a yankee could hide himself in. In the mean time we lay in the dark hole over the ceiling and trembled for our fate should we be discov-

ered.   A few other officers were concealed in the same garret,
awaiting events.

Night came at last, dark and dreary. About midnight
Devine and myself concluded to slip out of our hiding place
and inspect the premises. We went down. All was silent.—
There were no guards in the sentry-boxes on the high wall
around the camp. We took off our shoes and quietly crossed
over the dead-line to the wall, but it was too high to climb.—
With the aid of a scantling we happened to stumble over, I
managed to reach the top of the wall, when I beheld, not a
clear coast, but a line of guards on the ground, who evidently
were watching for us. I was discovered on the wall and they
were after us in a twinkling. In jumping from the wall I
dropped this diary from my clothes. The guard nearest us
came up into the sentry-box, and perhaps thinking we would
again attempt to scale the wall, stooped down in his box behind it, in order that he might shoot us should we attempt to
climb up. While he was in this position he could not see the
dead-line, so I crossed back, snatched up the papers and had
them safe.

The alarm was again raised, when a number of the guards
rushed into the prison swearing they had seen us, and should
they find us they would "be d——d if they didn't burn us
alive! We were then standing in one of the barracks near the
gate. The rebels thinking they had chased us under one of
the other cabins set fire to it to burn us up. They were terri-
bly exasperated, having been compelled to remain behind for
the sole purpose of catching a few "cussed yankees" who were
attempting to escape.

We knew if they found us our chance of life would be
very slim, so we determined to make a bold stroke, and if pos-

sible get outside the wall, which by this time was well guarded.
Pulling our old blankets around us, which made us look more
like rebels than yankees, we went out among the swearing
"Jonnies," gazed on the fire a moment, and then approached
the sentinel at the gate, saying the rebel Captain ordered us to
go out after buckets to carry water to put out the fire.

"All right," says the sentinel, "pass out."

And out we passed, when we saw another squad of sentinels in front of the gate. We ran by these, and in five minutes
were in the middle of Main street, marching into the city.—
Here we met a squadron of rebel cavalry, but a friendly cul-
vert under the street was near, and we dodged into it, while
they rode over us.

We were now out of prison, but what was to be done?—
We were in an enemy's city, filled with a great army, and daylight would certainly end our freedom.

There were but few lights in the city, and we approached
the one nearest us. Devine secreted himself while I inspected
it. It was certainly in a negro cabin, for I saw a black man
pass the window. I knocked and he came to the door. After
taking him into the garden I revealed myself, and asked his
assistance in our escape.

He was loyal, as all the blacks were, and replied: "Yes,
massa, I knows all about you. I'se seed you down dere in de
stockade many a time, and oh, how I'se pitied you!"

I knew now I was a free man!

His words fell on my ears like words from Paradise. He
was true, and would secrete us in his garret until Sherman's
army entered the city.

I slipped back to Devine and told him the glorious tidings. We would be free! A fellow bondman would loose our chains.

We both went back into the garden, and there, in the darkness, we seized that old slave's hand, and swore that while we lived our hands and our voices should ever be used in behalf of his oppressed race. We meant the words, and by the grace of God will keep them good!

The man's name was Edward Edwards.

He now helped us into his garret, and we felt safe.— He gave us a bed of straw, and we rested in sweet sleep till morning, and when we awoke, our faithful friend was there, waiting to give us food and water.

Sherman's army was now nearing the city, and a furious bombardment was going on. Many of the yankee shells came fearfully close to the cabin in which we were quartered.

Our colored friend now became our courier. We feared least Sherman might fail to take the city, and our escape thus be entirely foiled. We must know the news. How did the battle progress? and would the rebels evacuate the city?

So at least once an hour our friend would go up into the business part of the city and listen to the conversation of the rebels concerning the prospects, then hurry back and tell us what he had thus gleaned.

"They pears to be mighty gloomy, massa. They's hauling the cotton out into the streets to burn, and I thinks Mr. Sherman will take the city."

In the yard adjoining and immediately under our window (a little hole we had cut in the gable end of the house), were the quarters of the rebel General Chesnut. As the battle waxed warm, the general appeared very nervous, walking up and down the porch, giving orders to his aids and preparing to evacuate the city.

We could hear every word he said, and by his talk and movements were able to judge how the battle ebbed and flowed.

Little did he think two horrible yankees were close above his head chuckling over his sad appearance when he said to an aid, "Sherman has a bridge down, and will soon be over the river, and the game's up. We are whipped, and must leave the city."

His aids mounted and rode out of the city, followed by a small and sorrowful train of the general's military family.— The general came down into the yard, called one of his servants, bade her take good care of things, said "good-bye," took a long, last look at his home, and slowly rode away.

We now knew that our good time was coming. It was about noon of the seventeenth of February, 1865.

Shortly our old friend came running in, almost out of breath, and in his untutored eloquence cried, "Thank the Lord, the stars and stripes are waving over the Capital of South Carolina. Just look here and you can see 'em. Thank the Lord. Thank the Lord!"

We looked, and there was the dear old flag. We felt like shouting till the roof would raise from the house, but prudence taught us better, as some of the rebels were still passing down the street, out of the city, followed by the Federal cavalry.

"Friend Edwards, run up town and bring down a Federal soldier, and let us be certain that the city is ours," we exclaimed.

During his absence Devine and myself were shaking each others hands in mutual congratulation.

In a few minutes our friend came running in with an Iowa soldier. He grasped our hands and welcomed us back to freedom.

We immediately secured money and free passes for our more than friend, and hurried up into the city to meet the troops from God's land.

The 13th Iowa were first in the city, and had stacked arms in the street.

We saw the dear old flag, for which we had suffered so much, resting on the guns. We seized it, and with many a fervent kiss pressed it to our bosoms, thanking God that it had passed through all, victorious, unsullied and unstained.

An hour was passed in greetings among our friends on the streets, when General Sherman, attended by a magnificent cortege, entered the city.

The bands played "Hail Columbia," and a hundred flags fluttered in the breeze.

As Sherman came into the Main street, a tremendous shout from the soldiers fairly rent the heavens. It was "Sherman," "Victorious Billy Sherman."

Devine and myself, with two or three other prisoners who had also escaped, were standing on the stone steps of a store, gazing in wonder and admiration on the scene before us, when the General rode up and observing us, called us out, and shook us warmly by the hand, welcoming us back to liberty.

At this point Lieutenant Devine presented him the following song, which had been chanted so often in prison, and was now destined to a like honor from the grand old army that had marched with Sherman to the Sea.

WHAT I SAW IN DIXIE; OR,

SHERMAN'S MARCH TO THE SEA.

Oor camp fires shone bright on the mountains
  That frowned on the river below,
While we stood by our guns in the morning
  And eagerly watched for the foe—
When a rider came out from the darkness
  That hung over mountain and tree,
And shouted, "Boys up and be ready,
  For Sherman will march to the sea."

Then cheer upon cheer for bold Sherman
  Went up from each valley and glen,
And the bugles re-echoed the music
  That came from the lips of the men.
For we know that the stars in our banner
  More bright in their splendor would be,
And that blessings from Northland would greet us
  When Sherman marched down to the sea.

Then forward, boys. forward to battle,
  We marched on our wearisome way,
And we stormed the wild hills of Resaca,
  —God bless those who fell on that day—
Then Kenesaw, dark in its glory,
  Frowned down on the flag of the free,
But the East and the West bore our standards,
  And Sherman marched on to the sea.

Still onward we pressed, till our banners
  Swept out from Atlanta's grim walls
And the blood of the patriot dampened
  The soil where the traitor flag falls;
But we paused not to weep for the fallen,
  Who slept by each river and tree ;
Yet we twined them a wreath of the laurel
  As Sherman marched down to the sea.

O, proud was our army that morning
  That stood where the pine darkly towers,
When Sherman said : "Boys, you are weary,
  This day fair Savannah is ours."
Then sang we a song for our chieftain
  That echoed o'er river and lea,
And the stars in our banner shone brighter
  When Sherman marched down to the sea.

As the troops entered the city, the negroes met them with bottles and buckets of wine. All was rejoicing and excitement.

The rebel Wade Hampton, before leaving the city, had scattered hundreds of bales of cotton in the streets to be burned to prevent their falling into the hands of Sherman's army.— Many of the bales had been fired before he left the city, and were still burning, when about three o'clock a heavy wind rose and swept down the street of the city, almost blinding our eyes with dust and carrying the burning cotton to the roofs of many of the buildings.

Shortly after dark the horrible cry of "fire! fire! the city is on fire!" fell upon our ears. It was true; and now followed such a scene of terror as I hope never to see again. The boys, too, were spreading the conflagration by firing the city in a hundred places.

Lieutenant Devine and myself were stopping with a Union man on Main street, by the name of Cooper. He was a wealthy Philadelphian, who had lived in Columbia in luxury for some years. But this was to be his last day of wealth and ease, for the conflagration of that day made the old man a beggar.

When night came, many of our soldiers were intoxicated, and running through the streets yelling like madmen.

There were also prisoners, who had escaped from the enemy at different points, and some of them, infuriated by the hellish treatment they had received at the hands of the rebels, joined in the terrible scene.

Plunder was the order of the day, or rather of the night. Private residences and stores were burst open, and fired after being rifled of their most valuable contents. By nine o'clock at night the fire was at its height; the flames swept over the

streets and houses like a roaring torrent. Numbers of the intoxicated soldiers revelled in burning houses until the charred
walls fell in, when they perished beneath them. Old men sat
by their burning homes and wept; women, frightened into ma-
niacs, screamed in the streets.

It was a scene of terror, and there seemed no pity. Numbers of the citizens had carried their finest furniture—such as
pianos, etc., into the streets, to save it, when some soldier
would approach, sit down to an instrument, and by the light
of the burning houses, play the "*Devil's Dream.*" It was
Nero fiddling over burning Rome!

One woman, whose property I attempted to save from the
devouring element, lost her child; supposing it to be killed,
grew wild, and begged to be thrown into the flames—to be destroyed with her child. After an hour's search I found her
child, in the arms of a faithful negress, who had taken it to a
safe point to save it from the danger. I took it to the mother who, frantic with alarm, scarcely recognized her own lost
child.

The heat from the burning houses was almost intolerable.
I spent the greater portion of the night walking around the
city—witnessing the terrible events going on around me,—
The beautiful gardens, flowers, trees -and shrubbery, for which
the city was noted, were all destroyed. Churches, colleges
and cathedrals, were broken down, and daylight of Sunday
morning saw the city a black and smoking desert of ruins.

Around the charred ruins of their homes were grouped
whole families, mourning and weeping over the terrible desolation. Who could see it and not feel that Justice had been
avenged in this great curse on the city.

I sorrowed for the unfortunate innocents who were thus tumbled from opulence and luxury to worse than beggary, but for those who had caused it by their crimes, in my heart I had no pity. I only felt I saw—

"The Desolator desolate."

The army was soon on the move, again, for Cheraw, North Carolina, and I had found friends with that noble regiment—the Tenth Iowa.

My own regiment no longer existed as an organization. With killed, wounded and captured, there were few left of the brave one thousand, who had marched out from our gallant young Iowa at the Nation's call.

"Forth they came, a host of freemen,
From the setting of the sun.
Every hand was as a thousand—
While their hearts they were as one.

Long shall wave that starry banner,
That they bore so bravely on.
Long shall freemen point, in triumph,
To the battles they have won."

All who were captured from my Company, save one, died in Andersonville. Isaac Cartright lived to tell the sad story at home of our dear comrades. Isaac and David Loudenback, Matthew, William, and Jared Sparks, Daniel Bixler, and others, died, like Christian heroes, in that terrible slaughter pen. Brave and good men, all of them.

"But not in vain, they gave their spirits out—
Our Nation's life is sweeter for their blood."

Sixteen months ago, eighty of my Regiment were captured, and taken into Southern prisons. To-day, but *sixteen* of them live to tell the story.

Maj. Marshall made his escape, so did Captains Page and Bascom, and Lieutanants John and Mike Hoffman. They ran the guards, and reached our lines in East Tennessee.

I spent a few days with my friends in the Tenth Iowa, when Gen. Sherman sent for me, and, furnishing horse, saddle and tent, gave me a position, for the time, on his staff. I now had pleasant times, and I felt the contrast between starving in prison and living at the head quarters of a great army.

Sherman was now on his march back, through the Carolinas, and was at the head of the great and victorious army which marched with him to the sea. Every man was enthusiastic, and felt that victory could but follow when Sherman led. The General's appearance on the road, near a Division, was always the signal for loud and continued cheers "for Billy Sherman," and many were the instances, on that march, proving how devotedly the men were attached to their beloved commander.

Nor was that feeling thrown away upon Sherman, for he loved his army, and delighted to talk about his dear, brave boys, who rallied around his standard. No general—not excepting Napoleon—ever possessed so much of the great heart of an army, or was so idolized as Sherman, and he deserved it all. Afterwards, when certain officials and portions of the people, forgetting their great benefactor, refused to throw the mantle of charity over his seeming mistakes, they little thought how deeply they were wounding the hearts of the brave boys who loved him so well in spite of his errings.

Our army had captured Cheraw, with its forty cannon,

6

and all the prominent generals came to headquarters to rejoic over the victory.

Howard, "the Christian General," was there, and Johnny Logan, "the fighting General," Kilpatrick, the raider, with Corse, and a score of other stars, bright in the canopy of Mars, were there.

It was Sherman's military family, gathered in for a thanksgiving. They all rejoiced. Yet Sherman, even then, paced nervously up and down his quarters, his mind fixed on the future of the nation whose colors floated over a thousand camps before him.

Over the river, and a rapid march to Fayetteville, and that was ours, with its immense arsenals and vast quantities of munitions of war.

Dispatches were to be sent to General Grant and the President, and I was the lucky one to go. It was a hundred miles down Cape Fear River to the coast, and the rebels were on both sides. A small tug boat had run the blockade and joined us. In this boat, with a number of other soldiers, we ran down the river in the darkness of the night, and daylight found us in the city of Wilmington.

We steered down the harbor the next morning, and were transferred to the steamer Edward Everett. She was not laden, and my orders were to make no delay in reaching Gen. Grant, near the city of Richmond. By nine o'clock we sailed, under a stiff breeze, which increased to a gale towards night. We were off Cape Hatteras, and having no freight for ballast, our vessel could not ride the waves, but rocked like a bowl in the troughs between them.

I was sick. Oh! how sick! Numbers hung to the rail, and seemed to be throwing their stomachs out as offerings to

Neptune. The tables and chairs, broken from their fastenings, were on a grand high, chasing each other to and fro across the cabin floor. The dishes tumbled out at the pantry door, and to us "land-lubbers" it seemed terrible indeed.

The Captain swore, and the sailors worked calmly away, coiling and uncoiling the huge piles of rope, lifting the sails and picking up boxes, blocks, &c., which had been tumbled about by the storm.

Sundown brought a calm, and part of that night was spent in the steamer's cabin, dancing and singing songs.

At daylight we could see the dark walls of Fortress Monroe, and by noon a dispatch bearer from Sherman was announced to General Grant.

I was thanked for my promptness, and Grant was more than pleased over the success of his friend Sherman.

"And you want to go home, don't you?" said Grant.

"I should be most happy," I replied.

"Colonel," said the General, "give the Lieutenant free transportation to Washington, and a furlough to go home and remain as long as he wishes."

A brief glance at the army of the Potomac, and I was again steering down the James and up the Potomac to the city of Washington.

A week spent in seeing the sights in the Capital of the Nation was followed by an honorable discharge from the service, and I was off for my home in loyal Iowa,—a free man in a free land!

I had lived to see the glorious old flag, for which I had suffered so much, acknowledged the representative of the most magnanimous as well as most powerful nation on the face of the earth.

My service was done. I had served my country as I believed faithfully, and now I was to reap my reward in home, friends and peace,—yet willing and ready, should duty call, to again go, and if need be, sacrifice life itself to aid in maintaining the honor and dignity of our NOW FREE REPUBLIC

APPENDIX.

ANDERSONVILLE AS IT WAS AND IS.

A correspondent of the Boston *Journal* has faithfully told what Andersonville was and is, in the following account :

"Andersonville, to-day, presents a striking contrast to Andersonville of the "Confederacy." Then it swarmed with rebel troops and officers, and, with its stockades full to overflowing with human misery, and death reaping daily harvests from among the emaciated soldiers in the rude hospitals, looked little like the quiet village of to-day as it lies beneath the warm, pleasant sun of a Southern spring, with the gentle breeze dallying with the beautiful flag of the republic, as it floats from the staff in front of the office of the cemetery. No bayonet gleams from the sentry-boxes on the stockade or the dark red earthworks; no frowning muzzle of field artillery glowers from the embrasures of the battery, overlooking town and prisons; no swarms of hungry, half naked prisoners throng the hillsides; but all is quiet as death, except when the silence is broken by the passing train of cars or the echoing horn calling the workmen to and from their labors.

Within a distance of less than 1,000 yards of the railroad station, and due east from it, stands the "stockade," or, as it is often called, the prison pen." It is an inclosure, without a roof, about 2,000 feet long by 800 wide, and is built of logs from ten to twelve inches in diameter, set upright and close together in trenches about five feet deep. At about 100 feet from this is another stockade, which completely surrounds the other. This was built to prevent tunnelling, and as an additional obstacle in case of an outbreak of the prisoners. Around the top of the inner stockade, and at a distance of about sixty feet apart, are sentry-boxes, from which the guards can overlook their charges. About twenty feet from the base of the stockade was the "dead-line." Traces of this are still abundant, but the relic hunters are making inroads on it, and in a few years not a trace of it will be left.

The ground inside the stockade slopes down from the north and south towards a small stream, about five feet wide and six inches deep, which crosses the inclosure at right angles with its longest sides. Traces of the occupants still exist in the shape of mud and stick huts, mud chimneys, "burrows," rusty canteens, old shoes, beef bones, and such debris as usually remains in an old camp. Nine wells were dug by the prisoners, but the main supply of water was obtained from the stream; the tramp of so many thousand feet, and the filth of the ground, kept the water in a condition that rendered it altogether unfit for use. The water to-day is clear and beautiful.

South of the stockade, and about three hundred yards distant, is the hospital stockade, which surrounds fourteen open sided sheds like those in prison pen, with the exception of having mud and stick chimneys; but they are far better protected from the winter winds by their proximity to the stockade logs.

Directly to the west of the hospital stockade, and two thousand feet distant, stand the Confederate hospitals, two large frame buildings, well built and comfortable. These buildings are now occupied by freedmen's schools, and are under the immediate charge of Miss Mary S. Battey, of Providence, R. I. The school is carried on under the auspices of the American Missionary Association, and is very successful indeed.

Two hundred yards southeast from the railroad station is a small stockade, built for the confinement of Federal officers. This was mostly used for the confinement of citizens and turbulent rebel soldiers.

About 1,000 yards northwest from the prison pen, and about 1,200 from the railroad station, is the cemetery, in which are buried about 14,000 men. The first three hundred were buried in coffins, the next nine hundred were covered with boards and boughs, and from that number to 12,849 the bodies were buried shoulder to shoulder in trenches about three feet deep and six feet wide. About one thousand bodies have been brought here from Macon, Americus, Columbus, Eufaula, Albany, and other points in the vicinity.

The various States in the Union are represented in the cemetery as follows: Alabama, 16; Connecticut, 291; Delaware, 45; District of Columbia, 14; Illinois, 910; Indiana, 624; Iowa, 216; Kansas, 5; Kentucky, 456; Louisiana, 1; Maine, 282; Maryland, 194; Massachusetts, 774; Michigan, 606; Minnesota, 60; Missouri, 112; New Hampshire, 144; New Jersey, 170; New York, 2,534; North Carolina, 17; Ohio, 1,074; Pennsylvania, 1,825; Rhode Island, 74; Tennessee, 780; Vermont, 240; Virginia, 279; Wisconsin, 254; United States Army, 548; United States Navy, 99. Six men who murdered the sick were hung by their comrades. They were buried separate from the others. Three women were discovered among the prisoners and are buried among the soldiers. Each body in the cemetery has a numbered stake, with regiment, etc., and the date of death. The cemetery is on a level place of ground, and is, in some places, soft and sinking.

The climate in the region of Andersonville is very warm indeed, but the town is considered one of the most healthful in this part of the State. This I know is not the idea at the North, but it is easy to prove it by the old inhabitants and by records kept at the place. The enormous mortality at the pen is due to other causes. Of the large number of rebel soldiers kept as a garrison here, less than one hundred are buried in the vicinity.

List of Officers,

OF UNITED STATES ARMY AND NAVY, CONFINED AT COLUMBIA, SOUTH CAROLINA.

STATE OF NEW-YORK.

NAME.	RANK.	NAME.	RANK.
Aldrich, C. S.	Captain.	Butts, L. A.	Lieut.
Avery, W. B.	do	Bascomb, R.	do
Allstaedt, C. L.	Adj't.	Bath, W.	do
Ahlert, T. A.	Lieut.	Brandt, C. W.	do
Allen, S.	Captain.	Baker, H. E.	do
Adams, S. B.	do	Bennett, B.	Captain.
Andrews, S. T.	Lieut.	Bigley, C. H.	Lieut.
Abbett, A. O.	do	Burns, M.	do
Auer, M.	Captain.	Brown, C. A.	do
Brown, T. A.	do	Bospord, W. R.	do
Bradley, A. B.	R. Q. M.	Buchanan, W.	do

NEW-YORK — *Continued.*

NAME.	RANK.	NAME.	RANK.
Bryant, I. W.	Captain.	Clyde, J. D.	Captain.
Burrows, S. W.	Lieut.	Cole, A. F.	do
Bath, H.	do	Clark, L. S.	do
Beadle, M.	do	Cartwright, A. G.	do
Blane, W.	do	Coats, H. A.	do
Brickenhoff, M.	do	Coglin, T.	do
Bliss, A. T.	Captain.	Cloadt, J.	do
Barringer, A.	Lieut.	Case, D. L.	Adjutant.
Blasse, Wm.	do	Cook, E. F.	Major.
Burton, R.	Lt. & b. c.	Crooks, S. J.	Colonel.
Beebe, H. E.	do	Coffin, J. A.	Lieut.
Casler, B. G.	Captain.	Coover, J. H.	do
Campbell, L. A.	Lieut.	Cunningham, M.	do
Cromack, S. O.	do	Cramer, C. P.	do
Cornell, C. H.	do	Dietz, Henry	Captain.
Cutter, C. H.	do	Downing, O. J.	do
Chapin, H. A.	do	Derrickson, J. G.	do
Cahill, W.	do	Dusbrow, W.	do
Casler, J. L.	do	Duzenburgh, A.	do
Cooper, A.	do	Dixon, A.	do
Curtis, G. M.	do	Dunn, J.	Lieut.
Caslin, C. S.	do	Dunning, A. J.	do
Cain, J. H.	do	Davidson, J.	do
Clark, J. W.	do	Drake, I. W.	do
Casey, J.	do	Davis, J. W.	do
Canney, W. H.	do	Durboyne, G.	do
Cameron, P.	do	Erickson, J. H.	do
Curtiss, H. A.	do	Fatzer, S.	do

NEW-YORK — *Continued.*

NAME.	RANK.	NAME.	RANK.
Fauz, M	Captain.	Herzbery, F	Lieut.
Funk, I. W	do	Heury, T. M	do
Fisk, W. M	do	Hock, A	Captain.
Field, A	do	Heil, J	do
Fay, S. A	Lieut.	Hartzog, R. H. O.	do
Frost, C. W	do	Hoyt, H. B	do
Foote, M. C	do	Hayes, E	do
Faye, E. M	do	Hock, R. B	do
Fitzpatrick, L	do	Hamlin, S. G	do
Faass, Louis	do	Hendrick, F	do
Gilbert, E. C	Captain.	Hedges, S. P	Adjutant.
Gill, A. W. H	do	Hall, W. P	Major.
Getman, D	do	Irsch, F	Captain.
Goodrich, A. L	do	Johnson, V. W	Lieut.
Grant, H. D	Lieut.	Jones, S. E	do
Gilmore, J. A	do	Jones, D	Captain.
Granger, C. M	do	Judson, S. C	do
Glazeer, W. W	do	Johnson, B	do
Gottsland, C	do	Kankel, E	Lieut.
Goodrich, J. O	Adjutant.	Krohn, P	do
Hinds, H. C	Lieut.	Kennedy, J. W	do
Herrick, L. C	do	Kandler, H	do
Hastings, G. L	do	Kerley, M. W	do
Hauf, N	do	Kromemeyer, C	Captain.
Hopper, J	do	Lindemeyer, L	do
Hamilton, H. E	do	Lucas, W. D	do
Hezelton, D. W	do	Langworthy, D. A.	do
Hamilton, H. N	do	Lamson, A. T	Lieut.

98

WHAT I SAW IN DIXIE, ETC.

NEW-YORK.—*Continued.*

NAME.	RANK.	NAME.	RANK.
Lewis, C. E.	Lieut.	Merritt, H. A. D.	Lieut.
Lyman, H. H.	do	Murphy, J.	do
Lee, A.	do	Malleson, J.	do
Latter, J. A.	do	McHenry, C.	do
Leonard, A.	do	Merry, W. A.	do
Lemon, M. W.	do	McCormick, J.	do
Leith, S.	do	McLeman, P.	Major.
Locklin, A. W.	do	Miller, F. C.	Colonel.
Mussel, O.	Captain.	Nelson, P.	Major.
Murphy, F.	do	Nolan, H. J.	Captain.
Mooney, A. H.	do	Nyee, W.	Lieut.
McFadden, W. M.	do	Nelson, A.	do
Moore, N. H.	do	Norwood, J.	do
Mead, S.	do	Olcott, D. W.	Captain.
Manley, J. A.	do	O'Hara, J.	Lieut.
Mills, V.	Lieut.	Powers, J. L.	do
McDade, A.	do	Partridge, W. H.	do
Morand, F.	do	Pitt, G. W.	do
Mendenhall, J. A.	do	Pentzell, D.	do
Mell, J. R.	do	Pierson, M. P.	do
Mather, F. W.	do	Pitt, J. H.	do
Mockrie, P. B.	do	Palmer, E. L.	do
McCutcheon, E./T.	do	Peck, W. D.	do
McWain, E. J.	do	Pemberton, H. V.	Captain.
Morey, H.	do	Porter, E.	do
Myers, W. H.	do	Powell, J. P.	do
McKeehan, J. L.	do	Paine, L. B.	do
Mitchell, H. W.	do	Pettit, G.	do

NEW-YORK—*Continued.*

NAME.	RANK.	NAME,	RANK.
Pierce, S C.	Captain.	Schull, G.	Lieut.
Porter, B. B.	do	Schurr, C.	do
Payne, L. S.	do	Stanford, S. A.	do
Penfield, J. A.	Major.	Stuart, C.	do
Rockwell, W. O.	Lieut.	Shanan, M.	do
Rockwell, J. O.	do	Shelton, W. H.	do
Roach, W. E.	do	Sweet, W. H. S.	do
Raymond, H. W.	do	Smith, C. B.	do
Rothe, H.	do	Sultter, C.	do
Richardson, J. A.	do	Shaffer, H. C.	do
Riley, W. L.	do	Smith, L. S.	do
Reynolds, W. H.	Major.	Starr, H. P.	do
Ritter, H.	Captain.	Stebbins, J.	do
Ryder, S. B.	do	Stewart, R. R.	do
Reed, —	do	Schulter, H.	do
Reir, Geo. W.	do	Tuthill, P. A.	do
Reynolds, B. J.	do	Tainter, S. H.	do
Snyder, J.	do	Terwilliger, J. E.	do
Starkweather, W. L	do	Tompkins, H. V.	do
Star, G. H.	do	Temple, H.	do
Spring, W.	do	Tobel, C.	do
Stone, D.	do	Thorp, T. J.	Lt. Col.
Stevens, J. R.	do	Thompson, S. C.	Captain.
Swan, E. J.	do	Von Keiser, A.	do
Seeley, H. B.	Adjutant.	Vandeshif, J. W.	do
Scripture, F. E.	R. Q. M.	Van Buren, G. M.	do
Sears, D. C.	Lieut.	Von Haack —	do
Smith, J. A.	do	Veltfort, Geo.	Lieut.

NEW-YORK—*Continued.*

NAME,	RANK.	NAME,	RANK.
Vinay, F.............	Lieut.	Whiteside, J. C.......	Captain.
Von Rottenburg, H. N	do	Wentworth, H. A.	do
Van Rensaalaer, C	do	Wilson, M. C........	do
West, O. W.........	do	White, H. G.........	do
Wheeler, J. F......	do	Williams, E. H......	do
Wing, G. H.........	do	Walpole, H. H......	do
Woodruff, F. M.....	do	Walls, H. W.........	do
Willis, H. H........	do	Wanzer, G. G......	Major.
Warchaw, F.........	do	Young, J. W.........	do
Welch, J. C........	do	Yaw, E. C...........	Lieut.
Wilcox, W. H. H.	do	Zobel, C..............	do
Whittemore, B. W.	do		

STATE OF IOWA.

NAME,	RANK.	NAME,	RANK.
Austin, J. W.........	Lieut.	Dillon, C. D.........	Lieut.
Anderson, C. S......	do	DeLay, R...........	do
Byers, S. H. M......	Adj't.	Doane, E. B.........	Captain.
Bennett, W. F......	Captain.	Godley, M. L........	Lieut.
Brown, J. H........:	do	Huffman, J. W......	do
Conrad, W. F......	do	Haight, I. T.........	do
Clark, M. W........	do	Hoyt, W. H.........	do
Cassell, E. F.........	Lieut.	Irwin, S. E.........	do
Charters, A. M......	do	Kirkpatrick, G. W.	do
Cook, L. L...........,	do	Laird, M.............	do
Coddington, I. P.....	Vet. Surg.	McConalee, W. J....	do

IOWA — *Continued*.

NAME,	RANK.	NAME,	RANK.
Marshall, W. S.	Major.	Septon, A. F.	Lieut.
Morrisey, G. H.	R. Q. M.	Timm, A.	do
Parker, J. T.	Lieut.	Tower, D. W.	do
Purcell, T.	do	Thomson, F.	do
Page, J. E.	Captain.	Turner, J. H.	Captain.
Peckeville, W. F.	do	Tipton, A. F.	do
Ping, T.	do.	Waidmann, F.	Lieut.
Rorick, D.	Lt. A. D. C.	Woodrow, C. W.	do
Sanders, A. H.	Lt. Col.	Wright, J. W.	do
Smith, J. H.	Captain.	Warren, D. H.	Ass't Surg.
Shurtz, F.	do	Zimm, A.	Lieut.

STATE OF OHIO.

NAME,	RANK.	NAME,	RANK.
Alters, J. B.	Captain.	Brandt, O. B.	Lieut.
Alban, H. H.	do	Brush, Z. T.	do
Alger, A. B.	Lieut.	Barnes, O. P.	do
Acker, G. D.	do	Blae, J. G.	do
Anderson, R. W.	do	Blaire, Geo. E.	do
Armstrong, T. S.	do	Byron, E.	Captain.
Adams, H. W.	do	Bending, N. R.	do
Abbott, E. A.	do	Blinn, L. B.	do
Affleck, E. T.	Adj't.	Barrett, D. W.	do
Brown, W. H.	Lieut.	Bostwick, N.	do
Beard, J. V.	do	Blair, B. F.	Adj't.
Bailey, O. W.	do	Cusac, I.	Captain.

OHIO — *Continued*

NAME,	RANK.	NAME,	RANK.
Catin, M.	Captain.	Fairbanks, I	Lieut.
Canfield, S. S.	do	Fish, G W	do
Case, F. S.	do	Fowler, J H	do
Cutler, J.	do	Forney, D	do
Copeland, J. R.	do	Fairfield, O B	do
Clancey, C. W.	Lt. Col.	Fox, G B	Major.
Cook, A. A.	Lieut.	Green, J H	Lieut.
Culver, F. B.	do	Gross, C M	do
Corothers, J. J.	do	Goodin, A	do
Claghorn, A. C.	do	Gallagher, J	do
Cottingham, E.	do	Gatch, O C	Captain.
Carpenter, S D	do	Glen, S A	do
Cline, D J	do	Grafton, B	do
Caldwell, D B	do	Gates, J	do
Davis, L R	do	Hestler, J. W.	Captain.
Doughton, O G	do	Heer, T. A.	do
Dick, L	do	Heinrod, P.	do
Dickey, M V	do	Hallenburg, G.	Lieut.
Davidson, J W	do	Hare, T. H.	do
Davis, L R	Captain.	Henry, C. D.	do
Davenport, T F	do	Hays, W. W.	do
Dirlin, C. L	do	Hall, R. F.	do
Day, E	do	Hine, J. J.	do
Evans, B W	do	Hull, G. W.	do
Eberheart, M H	do	Harrison, C. E.	do
Eglin, A R	do	Hull, G. W	do
Edminston, S	Lieut.	Hackott, A. N	do
Francis, J L	Captain.	Hale, G. W	do

OHIO — (Continued.)

NAME.	RANK.	NAME.	RANK.
Imbrie, L. M.	- Captain.	Moore, Le Roy,	- Captain.
Jemmings, I. T.	do	Melkorn, ——	do
John, E. P.	- Lieut.	Moore, L.	do
Jones, J. P.	do	Nuhfer, A.	do
Jones, W.	do	Norris, O P	- Lieut.
Kelly, D. O.	do	Ouscolt, R V	do
Kerr, S. C.	do	Oats, J G	do
Kelly, A.	do	O'Sullivan, F G	do
Knowles, R. A.	do	Ogan, H W	Captain.
Knapp, F. A.	do	Piper, S B	Adj't.
Kennuly, J. D.	do	Pumphry, J B	Lieut.
Kempton, J. F.	do	Potts, J H	do
Kline, D. J.	do	Peetrey, J G	do
King, M. D.	do	Purtier, H	do
King, Abe,	do	Patterson, J B	do
Kepheart, J.	do	Paul, J S	do
McCune, A. W.	do	Patrec, L B	do
McNeil, S.	do	Patterson, G W	do
Mahoney, J. S.	do	Price, J C	do
Malamore, J M	do	Perrin, Z	do
McKinley, J	do	Palmer, J H	do
Mann, G	do	Rees, M	do
Maxwell, C A	do	Robinson, G L	do
McColgin, J	do	Retiley, W L.	do
McMahon, E	do	Ray, T J	do
McBeth, N	do	Reynolds, W J	Captain.
Marshall, J. D	do	Randolph, J T	do
Morgan, Benj. B	- Lt. Col.	Robbins, A	do

OHIO—(Continued.)

NAME,	RANK.	NAME,	RANK.
Rosenbaum, O H :	do	Taylor, A A :	: Lieut.
Rossman, W G ; ;	do	Thomas, D :	: Major.
Rings, G : :	: Adj't.	Thompson, J J T	: Ass't Surg.
Ring, A : ; :	: Lieut.	Tibbles, H G	: Captain.
Robinson, B E : :	do	Thomson, J :	: do
Rathbone, T W :	do	Underwood, J W	; do
Roney, J C : ; :	do	Ullenbaugh, G	; Lieut.
Sibby, H L : : :	do	Ulem, J ;	; do
Smith, M R : :	do	VanDoren, D ;	; do
Schuyler, J F : :	do	Winters, J ; .	; do
Spafford, A C : : ·	do	Welker, H W ;	; do
Spencer, F : :	do	Weatherbee, J ;	; do
Shaw, J C : : :	do	Weakly, T J ;	; do
Shepard, E : :	do	Watson, J C ;	; do
Spring, S : : ;	do	Whiting, J D ;	; do
Stout, J G ; : :	do	Wolbach, A R ;	; do
Stover, A C : :	do	Wiltshire, J W ;	; do
Stribling, M W : :	do	Weddle, Geo ;	; do
Shepstrong, M N :	do	Winner, C N ;	; do
Sutherland, O W : Adj't.		Wasson, J M ;	; do
Sheppard, E A : : Captain.		Westbrook, U S ;	; Captain.
Skilton, A S : : :	do	Wilson, W M Jr ;	do
Shutts, W : : : .	do	Wilson, J ; ;	; do
Singer, O P : : :	do	Williams, R ;	; do
Swayzie, W A : :	do	Wright, B J ; ;	; do
Stanbury, M L : :	do	Wallace, J ; ;	; Lt. col.
Shoemaker, F M :	do	Walker, W H ;	; Lieut.
Snodgrass, J C : :	do	Whitney, J De W ;	do
Theusen, B B : : Lieut.		Yontz, H C ; ;	; Captain.

8*

STATE OF PENNSYLVANIA.

NAME,	RANK.	NAME,	RANK.
Albaugh, Wm...	Captain.	Bryan, G.........	Adjutant.
Arthura, S. C.....	do	Burrett, J. A...	Captain.
Albright, J......	do	Bayard, G. A.....	do
Avery, W.........	do	Borchess, L. T..	do
Alexander, A. H.	do	Baker, W. F......	do
Anderson, J. F...	Lieut.	Chalfant, J. T....	do
Bricker, W. H...	do	Clark, M. L......	do
Bryson, R. R.....	do	Compher, M. L.	do
Burns, S. D......	do	Cratty, E. G......	do
Bierbower, Wm.	do	Crosby, T. J......	do
Beegle, D. F.....	do	Conyngham, J. B	Lieut. Col.
Bryon, J. H......	do	Cook, A. L........	Lieut.
Boone, S. G......	do	Cunningham, J..	do
Burns, J..........	do	Coslett, C........	do
Barton, J. L......	do	Crawford, C. H..	do
Barkley, C........	do	Crossley, S........	do
Burkholder, D W	do	Carlisle, L. B.....	do
Breon, J..........	do	Chambers, J. H.	do
Borchess, T. F...	do	Cope, J. D........	do
Brown, G. L......	do	Carter, W. H.....	do
Boughton, S. H.	do	Campbell, W. F.	do
Biller, S. N......	do	Cameron, J. F...	do
Bittenger, C. L.	do	Chatburn, I......	do
Braidey, A. J...	do	Cook, W. B......	do
Bick, W. C......	Captain.	Camp, T. B......	do
Bowers, G. W...	do	Creps, F. A......	do
Benner, H. S.....	do	Cubbison, J. C...	do
Byrns, J. M......	do	Cockran, T. G...	do

PENNSYLVANIA — *Continued.*

NAME,	RANK.	NAME,	RANK.
Carpenter, J. D.	Lieut.	Filler, J. H.	Major.
Catlin, E. I.	do	Fluke, A. L.	Lieut.
Cashell, E. P.	do	Fontaine, J.	do
Carpenter, E. N.	Captain.	Floeger, G. W.	do
Donaghy, J.	do	Flagan, E. A.	do
Daily, W. A.	do	Fellows, N.	do
Dinsmore, A.	do	Fontaine, F.	do
Dushane, J. M.	do	Gotshall, J.	do
Donohey, G. B.	do	Grant, G. G.	do
Dibeler, J. B.	do	Gamble, N. P.	do
Dewees, J. H.	Major.	Garbet, ——	do
Diffenbach, A. E.	Lieut.	Gordon, N. M.	do
Dean, S. V.	do	Gray, I. P.	do
Dotton, W. G.	do	Grey, Phillip.	do
Dodge, H. G.	do	Gray, W. L.	Captain.
Devine, J. S.	do	Greene, E. I.	do
Dieffenbach, w. H	do	Gimber, N. E.	do
Drake, E. H.	do	Guy, F. I.	do
Davis, Byron.	do	Graham, I P.	do
Eastman, F. R.	do	Heffley, A.	do
Evans, T. E.	do	Huff, A. B.	do
Evans, N. E.	Captain.	Hart, G. D.	do
Freeman, D W D	do	Haines, E. A.	do
Fahs, J. I.	do	Hogeland, D. B.	do
Farr, M. V.	do	Huey, Pennock.	Colonel.
Fraiser, J.	Colonel.	Hinds, E. E.	Lieut.
Filler, J. H.	Major.	Helm, J. B.	do
Flick, N.	Lieut.	Heffley, C. P.	do

PENNSYLVANIA— *Continued.*

NAME,	RANK.	NAME,	RANK.
Hubbell, E. A.	Lieut.	Keen, J.	Lieut.
Heffner, O.	do	Kreiger, A.	do
Harrington, B F	do	Kidder, G. E.	do
Hodge, J. F.	do	Knox, G.	do
Heslit, J.	do	Kelly, J I	do
Hazel, E I.	do	Kellow, J.	do
Herbert, I.	do	Keister, I.	do
Heppard, T.	do	King, T.	R. Q. M.
Horton, S L.	do	Kelly, E. L.	Captain.
Hart, C M.	do	Krause, J.	do
Hand, G T.	do	Kings, S. B.	do
Halpin, G.	do	Little, J. S.	do
Hagenback, J. T	do	Lytle, E. F.	do
Holohan, T. P.	do	Lynch, E. J.	Major.
Hewitt, J.	do	Longnecker, J H	Adjutant.
Harvey, J. L.	do	Laycock, J. B.	Lieut.
Hallet, M. V. B.	do	Lynn, J. L.	do
Hays, C. A.	do	Loud, E. DeC.	do
Haines, A. A.	do	Ludwey, M. S.	do
Hurst, T. B.	do	Lewry, D. W.	do
Irwin, W. E.	Adjutant.	Laughlin, J. M.	do
Johnson, J. C.	Captain.	Leslee, J. L.	do
Jobe, B. A.	do	Luther, J. T.	do
Jackson, C. G.	do	Lewis, D. B.	do
Jones, Alfred	Lieut. Col.	Myers, T.	do
Jones, E. E.	Lieut.	Mooney, J.	do
Justus, J. E.	do	Morningstar, H.	do
Krepps, F. A. E.	do	Marsh, P.	Captain.

PENNSYLVANIA — *Continued.*

NAME.	RANK.	NAME.	RANK.
McNeal, D.	Lieut.	McNitt, R. J.	Captain.
McGovern, J.	do	Millard, n. J.	do
McNicce, A.	do	Newlin, C.	do
Moore, F.	do	Norris, J.	do
Monaghan, J.	do	Norris, A. W.	Lieut.
McIntosh, I. C.	do	Neher, W.	do
Mangus, H. F.	do	Nisuander, D. M.	do
McLaughliu, I.	do	O'Connor, W.	do
McKay, D. S.	do	O'Shea, E.	do
Mayer, L.	do	O'Connell, P.	do
McCall, O.	do	Paxton, W. N.	do
Morrow, J. M.	do	Potts, G. P.	do
Morton, G. C.	do	Phelps, L. D.	do
Mason, J.	do	Potter, H. C.	do
Marshland, A. J.	do	Phillips F.	do
McNure, A.	do	Post, Jas.	do
McCreary, D. B.	Lieut. col.	Phillips, W. B.	do
McDowell, J. S.	Captain.	Piggott, J. T., Jr.	Captain.
McHugh, J.	do	Pennypacker, E.J.	do
McCray, H.	do	Robinson, W. A.	do
McKuge, J.	do	Richards, R. C.	do
Muffley, S. F.	do	Rose, W. B.	Lieut.
Marsh, L.	do	Ruger, J. M.	do
Metzger, J.	do	Rounela, J. R. A.	do
McCullin, D. W.	do	Rienockary G.	do
Mackey, F. J.	do	Rahu, Oro.	do
Morrow, J. J. H.	do	Robbinson, J. F.	do
Moses, O. C.	do	Ruff, Jas.	do

PENNSYLVANIA—Continued.

NAME.	RANK.	NAME.	RANK.
Roger, J. R.	Lieut.	Schooley, D.	Captain.
Riley, I. H.	do	Smullin, F.	do
Ruby, W.	do	Schell, G. L.	do
Sturgeon, W. H.	do	Schroade, I. E.	do
Stover, M. H.	do	Schofield, E.	do
Sweetland, A. A.	do	Stewart, R. T.	do
Shafer, W. H.	do	Scudder, A. A. R. Q. M.	
Stallman, C. H.	do	Templeton, O. F.	Captain.
Stroman, C. P.	do	Tyler, L. D. E.	do
Simpson, G. W.	do	Trout, I B.	Lieut.
Smith, J.	do	Thayer, E. O.	do
Shaefer, Jas.	do	Thompson, R. L.	do
Spence, D. M.	do	Taylor, E.	do
Stoke, G. W.	do	Urwiles, S.	Captain.
Stevens, F.	do	Van Allen, W. T	Lieut.
Snowwhite, E. E.	do	Weeks, E. I.	do
Sutler, J. R.	do	Weaver, E Z.	do
Sharp, G. A.	do	Wilson, E.	do
Smith, I. P.	do	White, A. B.	do
Stevens, I. G.	do	Warwick, Jas. F.	do
Sailor, I.	do	Welsh, N. E. E.	do
Smith, E.	do	Webb, G.	Captain.
Stauber, Benj. F.	do	Widdess, E. E.	do
Seeley, L. D.	do	Webb, Geo I.	do
Stevens, Frank.	do	Wenrick, E.	do
Steele, J.	Major.	Whittaker, E. B.	do
Speece, L. B.	do	Young, A. J.	Lieut.
Smart, G. F. C.	Captain.	Zeigler, Aaron	do
Smith, H. I.	do	Zarracher, F. K.	Captain.

STATE OF TENNESSEE.

NAME,	RANK.	NAME,	RANK.
Allender, W. F.	Lieut.	McIniddy, ——	Captain.
Adkins, P	do	Martin, J	do
Brown, W. L	do	Marney, A	do
Bishop, F. P	do	McDonald, J	Lieut.
Burdick, E. D	Captain.	Ottinger, W	do
Beal, E	do	Poston, J. L	do
Carnes, W. C	do	Robinson, J. L	do
Center, A. P	do	Reynolds, E. P.	do
Carroll, E	Lieut.	Risedon, I	do
Dricks, E. S. F	Captain.	Robe, E F	do
Fritz, Jas	Lieut.	Robeson, J. S	do
Grover, "Jep."	Major.	Smith, A	do
Geasland, S. A	Lieut.	Smith, P	do
Hawkins, S. W.	do	Smith, T. A	Major.
Huey, R	do	Stover, J	Captain.
Hagler, J. S	Captain.	Smith, D. D	do
Hays, A. I	do	Senter, A. P	do
Holt, E F	do	Underdown, J D	do
Kelley, J. M	Lieut.	Wiley, D	do
Lintz, D I	do	Walker, J	Lieut.
Lenter, A. P	Captain.	Wallace, J. J	do
Moore, G. W	do	Whittaker, F. D	do

STATE OF INDIANA.

NAME,	RANK.	NAME,	RANK.
Adair, W. A	Lieut.	Bush, James N.	Lieut.
Albin, H. S	do	Butler, E	do
Alden, G	do	Brownell, F. G.	do

INDIANA — *Continued.*

NAME.	RANK.	NAME	RANK.
Butler, T. H	Colonel.	Green, G W	Captain.
Burch, J	Captain.	Gude, A	do
Beebe, E D	do	Harvey, Wm H	Lieut.
Booher, A E	Lieut.	Hart, P H	do
Brown, James L	do	Hadley, H V	do
Barlow, J W	do	Hollander, V G	do
Chisman, E	do	Harris, I W	do
Chittenden, J L	do	Harris, G	do
Clegg, F	do	Hefflefinger, J	do
Carr, J P	do	Isett, J H	Major.
Carey, A A	do	James, H H	Lieut.
Dooley, A T	do	Jackson, J	do
Delane, J A	do	Knowles, E M	do
Dugan, I	do	Kane, S	do
Denny, W N	Captain.	Knox, J C	do
Davis, I B	do	Kepheart, J S	do
Durand, I	do	Kendale, W M	Major.
Eyestone, I W	Lieut.	Kessler, J G	Captain.
Elder, F I	do	Kendall, J	do
Fry, Alfred	do	Laud, J R	do
Fisher, S	do	Lamsom, T D	Lieut.
Finney, Geo E	Adjutant.	Lloyd, T S C	do
Fisher, S	Lieut.	Larkin, F A	do
Godown, I N	do	McGowan, E	do
Grover, J E	do	Messick, J M	do
Gamble, H	do	Makepeace, A J	Captain.
Gordon, E	do	Metcalf, C W	do
Green, C W	do	Matson, C C	Lieut. Col.

INDIANA — *Continued.*

NAME.	RANK.	NAME	RANK.
Moore, F.........	Captain.	Stanton, F.........	Lieut.
Mall, E. E.........	do	Shannon, Abe L	do
McHolland, D A	do	Sharp, E E......	do
McGrayles, L..	do	Smith, I E.........	do
Marshall, W S	Adjutant.	Simpson, I D......	do
Munday, I E......	Lieut.	Simmons, A E...	do
Murdock, H E...	do	Shaefer, N I......	do
Mills, I E.........	do	Spencer, T D A	Captain.
Mayer, G E.....	do	Schommerhone, I	do
Neal, A............	do	Smith, O J.........	Major.
Nulland, R......	do	Thompson, C H	do
Purveaner, J S	do	Tillottson, H H..	Lieut.
Parmaler, E A	Captain.	Thomas, A V......	do
Phelps, I D......	do	Taylor, A A......	do
Paine, A...........	do	Tinker, T I......	do
Russell, E.........	do	Uptgrove, P R	do
Richley, A.........	do	Van Ness, Geo A	do
Richardson, H A	Lieut.	Wright, D L......	do
Roach, A.........	do	Woodrow, I C D	do
Rugg, I L.........	do	Whitman, W S..	do
Rice, E S.........	do	Willis, W G......	do
Ross, E H.........	Adjutant.	Wakefield, H B	Captain.
Scott, Geo.........	Lieut.	York, J H......	Lieut.

STATE OF ILLINOIS.

NAME.	RANK.	NAME.	RANK.
Albro, S A......	Lieut.	Abernathy, H C	Adjutant.
Adams, Jas......	do	Allee, A A......	Lieut.

ILLINOIS — *Continued.*

NAME,	RANK.	NAME,	RANK.
Bassett, E E	Lieut.	George, G I	Lieut.
Benson, I F	do	Gamble, E S	do
Brunn, S	do	Griffin, T S	do
Beasley, I L	do	Green, E A	do
Basett, W E	do	Gore, S T	do
Briggs, E	do	Gross, T	do
Bryant, E E	do	Gerhardt, T	do
Boaz, E P	Captain.	Grey, T S	do
Bigelow, A I	do	Gutjaher, O	Captain.
Blanchard, Geo A	do	Hanley, T	do
Baker, A D	do	Hith, V R	do
Conover, S D	do	Hodge, A	do
Crawford, E P	do	Hay, D	do
Caswell, E	Lieut.	Hawkins, T E	do
Caldwell, E	do	Hymer, S	do
Cole, O S	do	Hubbard, R E	Lieut.
Counelly, R I	do	Hanon, I	do
Calkins, Wm W.	do	Harmer, S	do
Cox, I T	do	Hovey, N	do
Cunniffe, E	do	Hughes, R N	do
Channel, J R	do	Havens, D	do
Davis, T S	do	Howe, E N	do
Dorris, E E	de	Haldeman, Fred.	do
Davis, E I	do	Huntley, E. E	do
Fox, E	do	Hood, John	do
Fritze, O	do	Irwin, E S	do
Foster, E F	Captain.	Jones, I A	do
Gillespie, S B	do	Jones, S F	Captain.

ILLINOIS — *Continued.*

NAME,	RANK.	NAME,	RANK.
James, H H......	Lieut.	Porter, D M......	Captain.
Jackson, J.........	do	Pace, N S.........	do
Knowles, E M...	do	Porter, L..........	Lieut.
Kane, S............	do	Quigg, D..........	Major.
Knox, J C........	do	Roach, S............	Lieut.
Kepheart, J S...	do	Reynolds, T.......	do
Kendale, W M...	Major.	Randall, W.......	do
Lamsom, T D...	Lieut.	Rose, S. E.........	do
McGowan, E.....	do	Roberts, E R.....	do
Messick, J M.....	do	Reed, T S.........	do
Makepeace, A J	Captain.	Rice, J A.........	Captain.
Metcalf, C W.....	do	Rourke, S.........	do
Matson, C C......	Lieut. Col.	Russell, J A......	do
McDonald, C.....	Lieut.	Strang, O. T......	do
Main, S A.........	Captain.	Shedd, W.........	Colonel.
Miller, S..........	Adjutant.	Smythe, S. S......	Lieut.
Morris, M.........	Lieut.	Swift, E D.........	do
Newsome, E......	Captain.	Scoroeder, T V...	do
O'Kain, J.........	Lieut.	Stevens, G.........	do
Olden, E S......	do	Spindler, J.........	do
Picquet, S.........	do	Schwainforth, F.	do
Phinney, A.......	do	Sanger, A V......	do
Provine, W.......	do	Segar, T. R......	do
Powell, E.........	do	Strickland, E. P.	do
Parker, S..........	do	Scoville, T I......	Captain.
Powell, O.........	do	Suther, E. S......	do
Prather, Z B.....	do	Smith, A B........	do
Pain, T S.........	do	Sellick, R.........	do

ILLINOIS — *Continued.*

NAME.	RANK.	NAME	RANK.
Shroeder, H	Lieut.	Welshimer, P	Captain.
Tunner, D	do	Wright, V R	do
Turner, David	do	Young, D G	do
Worthen, T A	do	Young, W J	Lieut.
Winship, J	do	Yates, S T	do
Wilson, R	do	Zeis, H	Captain.

STATE OF WEST VIRGINIA.

NAME.	RANK.	NAME.	RANK.
Aheern, M	Lieut.	Kessler, J G	Captain.
Anshutz, H T	do	Kendall, J	do
Beebe, E D	do	Laud, J R	do
Chisman, E	do	Larkin, F A	Lieut.
Chittenden, J L	do	Lloyd, T S C	do
Clegg, F	do	Pickenpaugh, E I	do
Carr, J P	do	Phares, V	do
Carey, A A	do	Patterson, F. A.	Captain.
Carpenter, E. N.	Captain.	Phelps, L A	do
Cashell, E. P	do	Poole, J F	Lieut.
Eastman, F. R	do	Richard, J M	do
Gude, A	do	Robb, W. J	Captain.
Green, G W	do	Steel, J M	Lieut.
Hollander, V G	do	Smith, J B	do
Hart, P H	do	Williamson, J B	do
Hadley, H V	do	White, C W	Captain.
Jenkins, G W	Lieut.	White, G W	do

STATE OF VERMONT.

NAME,	RANK.	NAME,	RANK.
Adams, C A......	Captain.	Kenfield, F........	Lieut.
Boutin, C W......	do	Morton, I. T.....	do
Beman, V N.....	do	Morrow, I. M.....	do
Chapin, N S......	do	Meall, O...........	do
Carr, O P........	Lieut.	Needham, I B...	do
Correll, E........	do	Phillips, w. D.....	do
Chase, N R......	do	Post, Jas...........	do
Cuuningham, Ed	do	Phillips F.........	do
French, N........	do	Rohu, O..........	do
Fisher, L W......	do	Rieneckar, G.....	do
Fleming, E K.....	do	Smith, E B......	do
Grant, E...........	Captain.	Sargeant, M G.,.	do
Hart, E R........	Lieut.	Stone, E. P......	do
Holden, E.........	do	Stone, L L........	R. Q. M.
Holman, N R...	do	Schofield, R.......	Captain.
Higley, E N......	do	Thompson, J S...	Lieut.

STATE OF MICHIGAN.

NAME,	RANK.	NAME,	RANK.
Andrews, H B...	Captain.	Bremen, S.........	Captain.
Alexander, E. P.	Lieut.	Ballard, S N......	Lieut.
Abbey, A S........	do	Bateman, Wm...	do
Andrews, E E...	do	Barnard, R. A...	do
Button, G W...	do	Copeland, W. A.	do
Boyd, N R......	do	Clark, J. A......	Captain.
Barso, J R......	do	Colville, J. W.....	do

MICHIGAN—Continued.

NAME.	RANK.	NAME.	RANK.
Dafoe, T S	Captain.	Litchfield, A. O.	Lieut. Col.
Dodge, E E	do	McDowell, J. S.	Captain.
Dygert, 'Kin.' S.	do	McNure, A	do
Dicey, E E	do	Marshland, A. J.	do
Drake, S	Lieut.	Mason, J	do
Deane, T S	do	Muffley, S. F.	do
Dalton, G A	do	McKage, J	do
Ferris, S M	do	McCray, I	do
Frost, B I	do	McHugh, J	do
Grant, S	do	Norton, E E——	do
Gordon, George S	do	Nyman, N S	Lieut.
Greble, T E	Captain.	Potter, H. C.	do
Galbraith, H E	do	Phelps, L D	do
Goetz, I	do	Potts, G. P.	do
Hutchison, R. T.	do	Paxton, W. S.	do
Hill, Geo. W	Lieut.	Pennypacker, E J.	do
Harris, S	do	Piggott, J. T., Jr.	Captain.
Hurd, W. B	do	Pierson, A P	Lieut.
Hendryck, N V	do	Price, N S	do
Hamilton, N. T.	do	Rounds, J. B.	do
Hull, E T	do	Ruger, J. N.	do
Isham, A. B	do	Spaulding, E G.	do
Kellogg, N	do	Schofield, T D.	do
Knight, N B	do	Van Natter, R. N	do
Keeler, A M	Captain.	Williams, O	do
Logan, R. S	do	Willets, W	do
Lee, E. N	do	Williams, W	do
Lanning, A	Sergeant.	Warner, J B	do
Lombard, E G	Adjutant.	Wands, H. P.	Captain.

STATE OF MARYLAND.

NAME,	RANK.	NAME,	RANK.
Apple, H.	Lieut.	Hinds, E. E.	Lieut.
Berry, A.	Captain.	Haines, E. A.	do
Carpenter, J. D.	Lieut.	Krause, J.	do
Catlin, E. I.	do	Kelly, E. L.	Captain.
Donaghy, J.	do	Kidder, G. E.	do
Daily, W. A.	do	Knox, G.	do
Dinsmore, A.	do	Long, R. T.	do
Dushane, J. M.	do	Metta, I S.	do
Evans, N. E.	Captain.	Pelton, E.	do
Flick, N.	Lieut.	Socks, J.	do
Filler, J. H.	Major.	Sevcadner, Jas.	do
Gotshall, J.	do	Stewart, Thos. A.	do
Grant, G. G.	do	Schroeder, E.	do
Gamble, N. P.	do	Smyser, H C.	do

STATE OF RHODE ISLAND.

NAME,	RANK.	NAME,	RANK.
Aigin, John	Captain.	Fluke, A. L.	Lieut.
Booher, A E.	Lieut.	Fontaine, E.	do
Brown, James L	do	Garbet, ——	do
Barlow, J W.	do	Gordon, N. M.	do
Chase, E. E.	do	Hart, G. D.	do
Donohey, G. B.	do	Heffley, A.	do
Dibeler, J. B.	do	Sullivan, J.	Adjutant.
Dewees, J. H.	Major.	Sherman, S. U.	Captain.
Diffenbach, A. E.	Lieut.	Whitney, J. N.	Lieut.

STATE OF MASSACHUSETTS.

NAME.	RANK.	NAME.	RANK.
Adams, J G B...	Lieut.	Harvey, Wm H	Lieut.
Carey, S. F........	do	Helm, J. B........	do
Creasy, Geo. W.	do	Heffley, C. P....	do
Chubbuck, D. B.	do	Harris, I W......	do
Dean, S. V........	do	Harris, G.........	do
Dotton, W. G...	do	Hefflefinger, J...	do
Dodge, H. G......	do	Hogeland, D. B.	do
Devine, J. S......	do	Huff, A. B........	do
Dieffeubach, w. H	do	Huey, Pennock...	Colonel.
Drake, E. H......	do	Isett, J H.........	Major.
Davis, Byron.....	do	Kennits, H.......	Lieut.
Evans, T. E......	do	Kelly, J I	do
Eyestone, I W...	Captain.	Kellow, J.........	do
Filler, J. H......	Major.	Keister, I.........	do
Fisher, S.........	Lieut.	King, T............	R. Q. M.
Fry, Alfred......	do	Morton, J W...	Captain.
Fisher, S..........	do	May, J.............	do
Finuey, Geo E...	Adjutant.	McGinnis, J. W	do
Fontaine, J........	do	Moulton, O	Lieut. Col.
Fleeger, G. W...	do	Mullegan, Jas A	Lieut.
Flagan, E. A...	do	Moodey, J E......	do
Fellows, N........	do	McManus, P. W.	do
Gray, I. P.........	do	Manning, Geo A	do
Grey, Phillip.....	do	Narcross, J. S....	do
Gray, W. L......	Captain.	Nutting, J. H....	do
Greene, E. I......	do	Osborne, F I......	do
Gimber, N. E....	do	Platt, S H.........	do
Guy, F. I.........	do	Russell, J H......	do

120 WHAT I SAW IN DIXIE, ETC.

MASSACHUSETTS—*Continued.*

NAME,	RANK.	NAME,	RANK.
Reade, J	Lieut.	Sampson, I. B	Captain.
Sinclair, R B	do	Wilder, G O	Adjutant.
Sampson, I B	do	Whiston, D	Lieut.
Skinner, I T	do	Wilson, E. S	do
Swift, R R	do		

STATE OF MAINE.

NAME,	RANK.	NAME,	RANK.
Anderson, H. M.	Lieut.	Larrabee, W. H.	Lieut.
Blake,——	do	Litchfield, J B	Captain.
Bisbee, S T	do	Metzger, J	do
Bisbee, Geo. D.	do	Marsh, L H	do
Bixby, N P	do	Poindexter, E. O	do
Brown, T O	do	Richards, R. C	do
Bartlett, O E	do	Sargeant, H R	do
Coffin, V. S	do	Stevens, S N	Lieut.
Chandler, G A	do	Smith, M S	do
Childs, I W	do	Shelton, J P	do
Dearing, N A	do	Toby, J B F	do
Day, R. S	Captain.	Vaughn, Z	Captain.
Falls, F P	do	Willis, A R	do
Gordon, E O	Lieut.	White, Daniel	Colonel.
Gilman,——	do	Ware, Elton W.	Lieut.
Hunt, S O	do	Whitten, B F	do
Jackson, S T	do	Wadsworth, M.C	do
Jones, E F	do		

10*

STATE OF CONNECTICUT.

NAME,	RANK.	NAME,	RANK.
Andrus, W. R...	Lieut.	Koet, R...........	Lieut.
Bartram, D. S...	do	King, John........	do
Bowers, G. A.....	do	Landen, H........	do
Blakeslee, B. F..	do	Loomis, A. W...	do
Burns, H.........	do	Locke, W. H.....	do
Bristol, J. H......	do	Lindsy, A. H...	do
Bowen, C. D......	Captain.	Merwin, S. T. C.	do
Biebel, H.........	do	Matherson, E. J.	do
Burke, F. F......	do	McKeag, F......	do
Case, A. G.........	Lieut.	Miller, W. G......	do
Cowles, H. F......	do	Moree, C. W......	do
Carpenter, E. D.	do	McDonald, H. G.	Captain.
Clapp, J. B......	Adjutant.	Nichols, C. H...	do
Chamberlain, v.B	Captain,	Pasco, H. L......	Major.
Dennis, J. B......	do	Pierce, H. H......	Lieut·
Davis, H. C......	do	Phillips, W. E...	do
Dickerson, A. A	Lieut.	Strong, E. E......	do
Day, A. P.........	do	Sanford, O. L.....	Major.
Dyre, E. B......	do	Turner, M. C......	Captain.
Hobbie, C. A....	Captain.	Tourtillote, J.....	do
Hintz, A...........	do	Tyler, L. E......	Lieut.
Johnson, G........	Lieut.	West, D. J.........	do
Jordon, E. C......	do	Woodard, J. E...	do
Kees, G. W......	do	Wheeler, J. D...	Captain.

STATE OF KENTUCKY.

NAME,	RANK.	NAME,	RANK.
Arthur, J. A.......	Captain.	Adams, W. C.....	Lieut.

KENTUCKY — *Continued.*

NAME.	RANK.	NAME.	RANK.
Banks, B. V......	Captain.	Morris, J. H......	Lieut.
Coleman, S. S.....	Lieut.	Merrill, H. P.....	Captain.
Curtis, R...........	do	Nicmager, B. H.	Lieut.
Clements, J........	do	Owens, W. N.....	Major.
Cohen, M.........	Captain.	Pulliam, M. D...	Lieut.
Dillon, F. W......	do	Potter, G. A......	do
Dunn, H. C......	Lieut.	Riggs, B. T......	Captain.
English, D........	Major.	Rogers, A.........., ...	do
Gunn, T. M......	Lieut.	Sheerd, D. G......	Lieut.
Gross, J. M........	Captain.	Swope, C. T......	do
Heltemus, J. B....	do	Stewart, A. S.....	do
Jacobs, I, W.....	do	Scott, R. F........	do
Kelly, D. A......	do	String, T. B......	Captain.
Kautz, I. E......	Lieut.	Thornbury, J. M.	Lieut.
Lucas, John......	Captain.	Thorn, R. F......	do
Lovett, L. T......	do	Unthank, C. L...	Captain.
Lock, D. R........	Lieut.	West, J. H........	do
Moses, H...........	do	Williams, M. T..	Lieut.
Mead, W. H......	do	Young, T. B......	do

STATE OF NEW JERSEY.

NAME.	RANK.	NAME.	RANK.
Appleget, A. S...	Lieut.	Bradford, John..	Lieut.
Allen, Robert.....	do	Crocker, H........	do
Bulow, A.........	do	Donovan, J......	do
Baldwin, C. W...	do	Downs, C.........	do

NEW JERSEY —*Continued.*

NAME.	RANK.	NAME.	RANK.
Drake, J. M......	Lieut.	Kissam, Edgar...	Captain.
Elkin, J. L. F...	Adjutant.	Maltison, A. C...	do
Furgerson, J......	Lieut.	Oliphant, D......	Lieut.
Flannery, D......	do	Parker, J.........	Captain.
Fowler, H. M.....	do	Peters, G...........	Lieut.
Heston, H........	do	Romaine, L........	do
Johnson, J. D...	Captain.	Rainear, L........	do
Keudrick, E......	Adjutant.	Schwartz, L, S...	do

STATE OF MISSOURI.

NAME.	RANK.	NAME.	RANK.
Baker, S. S........	Lieut.	Kreuger, W......	Lieut.
Bader, H............	do	Muri, C............	do
Diemer, M........	do	Newbrant, J. F...	do
Driscoll, D........	do .	O'Brien, E........	Captain.
Fritchy, A. W...	do	Pyne, D. B........	Lieut.
Fisher, R.........	do	VonHelmrick, G.	Lt. Col.
Harris, W.........	Captain.	Whitney, M. G...	Captain.
Hescock, H........	do		

STATE OF WISCONSIN.

NAME.	RANK.	NAME.	RANK.
Baldwin, M. R...	Captain.	Butler, W. O.....	do
Botts, W. O......	Lieut.	Bennett, I.........	do

WHAT I SAW IN DIXIE, ETC.

WISCONSIN — *Continued.*

NAME,	RANK.	NAME,	RANK.
Collins, W. A......	Captain.	McKinson, H. H.	Lieut.
Carperts, L. M...	do	Munger, T. J.....	do
Caldwell, C........	Lieut,	McKercher, D...	Colonel.
Dahl, O. R........	do	McIntyre, ——..	Captain.
Dickerson, E.....	do	Ogden, J...........	Lieut.
Elliuwood, W. B	do	Prattsman, C. A..	do
Ewen, M...........	Captain.	Pope, W. A......	do
Fairchild, H......	Lieut.	Parsons, W. N...	Major.
Gates, A. L......	do	Perry, F. M.....	Captain.
Grant, A...........	Captain.	Robbins, H........	do
Hobart, M. C.....	do	Sandon, W........	Lieut.
Holmes, A. J.....	do	Western, C. S.....	do
Hull, C........:...	Lieut.	Warren, J. W...	do
Morgan, C. H.....	do	Watson, W. L...	do
McGruder, W. H	do		

STATE OF MINNESOTA.

NAME,	RANK.	NAME,	RANK.
Ford, E. W........	Captain.	McLane, —— ...	Lieut.
Hall, A. M........	Lieut.	Medenhoffen, C...	do
Lane, L. M......	do	Tiffany, A. W...	do
McCain, J. C.....	do		

STATE OF NEW HAMPSHIRE.

NAME,	RANK.	NAME	RANK.
Buckley, H........	Lieut.	Roberts, G.........	Lieut.
Duven, J...........	do	Tilbrand, H......	Captain.
Demmick, O. W.	do	Wilcox, C. W.....	Lieut.
Drew, G. H......	do		

MISCELLANEOUS.

NAME,	RANK.	NAME,	RANK.
Bartley, R.........	Lieut.	Love, J. E........	Captain.
Bischoff, P........	do	Molton, H.........	Lieut.
Brady, W. H.....	do	Montgomery, R H	do
Benson, A. N.....	Captain.	McCafferty, N. J.	do
Brown, S.........	A. M. M.	McClure, T. W.	do
Califf, B. F........	Lieut.	Murry, S. F......	Captain.
Conn, E............	do	Nash, w. H........	do
Dewees, T. B.....	do	Nolan, L...........	do
Eagan, John......	do	Perrin, J............	Adj't.
Edwards, T. D...	As'nt Eng.	Pettijohn, D. B...	Lieut.
Elder, S. S........	Captain.	Reid, J. A..........	do
Eastmond, O......	do	Spaulding, E. J..	do
Fielder, J.........	do	Shaffer, H. C......	do
Fortescue, L. R..	Lieut.	Stoughton, H. R.	Lt. Col.
Jones, H............	do	Wilson, R. P......	Lieut.
Keriu, J...........	do	York, E. D........	do

COLORED TROOPS.

NAME	RANK	NAME	RANK
Baird, Wm........	Lieut.	Hill, O. M.........	Lieut.
Bowley, F. S......	do	Latimer, E C......	Captain.
Beecham, R. K...	do	Mix, W. H........	Lieut.
Barnum, S. D....	Captain.	Raynor, A. J......	do
Caso, M. B........	Lieut.	Robinson, C.......	Captain.
Downing, H. A.	do	Shull, J. F.........	Lieut.
Daniels, E. S......	Captain.	Smith, S. B.......	do
Griffin, T...........	Adj't	Scott, D. W.......	Captain.
Hand, S. P........	Lieut.	Sanders, C. B.....	Lieut.

COLORED TROOPS— *Continued.*

NAME,	RANK.	NAME,	RANK.
Simondson, P. A.	Lieut.	Kendall, T.	do
Ward, T. H.	do	Laird, J. O.	do
Wheaton, J.	do	Murphy, J.	do
Christopher, J.	Captain.	Mackey, J. T.	do
Cochran, M. A.	do	Nelson, W, H.	do
Causten, M. C.	Lieut.	Noggle, C. L.	do
Cord, T. A.	do	Nealy, O. H.	do
Durnam, T. J.	do	Netlerville, W. M	do
Freeman, H. B.	do	Plase, W. B.	Captain.
Gray, R. H.	do	Pierce, G. S.	do
Gates, R. C.	do	Rowley, G. A.	Lieut.
Gageby, J. H.	do	Smythe, W. H.	do
Galloway,——.	do	Von Valack, D.D.	do
Hart, R. K.	Captain.	Teneycks, S.	do
Huntington, E. S	Lieut.		

Railroads.

BURLINGTON ROUTE

—To—

CENTRAL & SOUTHERN IOWA,

Via.

CHICAGO, BURLINGTON & QUINCY,

AND

Burlington & Missouri River R. R.

TWO Trains Daily between—

Chicago,
Burlington,
Ottumwa,
Osceola
DesMoines,

And Western Terminus of B. & M. R. R., where Connections are made with the Coaches of the WESTERN STAGE COMPANY.

☞Buy Tickets via. BURLINGTON.☜   Fare as low and time as quick as by any other route.

L. CARPER,   } Gen. Pass. Agent. {   C. E. PERKINS, Supt. B. & M. R. R.

Health Institution.

Our Home on the Hillside,

Danaville, Livingston Co., N. Y.

THIS Institution is the largest Hygienic Water Cure at present existing in the world. It is presided over by, and is under the medical management of, Dr. James C. Jackson, who is the discoverer of the Psycho-Hygienic method of treating the sick, and under the application of which he has treated nearly—

20,000 Persons!

In the last twenty years, with most eminent success, and *without giving any of them any Medicine.*

The Psycho Hygienic philosophy of treating the sick -no matter what their age, sex, or disease. consists in the use of those means only as remedial agencies, whose ordinary or legitimate effect on the human living body when taken into or applied to it, is to *preserve* its health. The fallacy of giving poisonous medicines to Invalids has been abundantly shown in Our Home in the results of our treatment.

Our Institution is large enough to accommodate 250 guests ; is, after the plan adopted by us, complete in all its appointments—having worthy and intelligent helpers in all its departments of labor, and who give their proportion of sympathy and influence to the creation and maintenance of a sentiment and opinion cheering to the Invalid, and therefore decidedly therapeutic in its effects.

THE SCENERY

About the Establishment is very beautiful, the air is dry and very salubrious ; we have plenty of sunshine, and pure, soft, living water in great abundance. Besides all these, and which we prize as one of the highest privileges and Health-giving opportunities our guests could possibly have. we live ourselves, and so can enable them to live, free from Fashion and her expensive and ruinous ways. Life with us is simple, not sybartic ; is true, not hollow and false,—and so of itself tends to its own perpetuation, and of course to health.

A great many of our guests who have for years been great sufferers,—growing steadily more and more sickly, begin to get well, and go on get ting well in such silent yet sure, in such imperceptible yet certain ways, as never to be conscious how it was brought about. The means used seem so utterly incommensurate to the results produced, that it seems marvelous. So true is it that in Nature

> " God's mightiest things
> Are His simplest things,"

and that to understand how things are done, one needs to cultivate a teachable spirit, and to cherish reverence for Law. To teach those who come to us for treatment what the laws of life are, and to awaken in them the desire to obey those laws, is to establish a most favorable condition precedent to their recovery.

Sick ones, whoever you are, or wherever you are, do you want to get well? And to learn how to keep your health, having got well? Come to Our Home if you can, and once here learn the all important lesson that—

> " Nature as a mistress is gentle and holy,
> And to obey Her is to live."

Circulars of the Institution,

Or any information in regard to it, may be obtained by addressing either James C. Jackson, M. D., Miss Harriet N. Austin, M. D., or Dr. James H. Jackson.

These Physicians may also be consulted by letter by the sick who are unable to attend the establishment.

Fee for home prescription, $5,00.

AUSTIN, JACKSON & CO.,
Proprietors.

HARRIET N. AUSTIN,
JAMES H. JACKSON,
LUCRETIA E. JACKSON. }

GALESBURG WATER CURE, OR HYGIENE HOME.

THE method of treating diseases adopted at this Institution is original with its Physician-in-Chief, and differs widely from the Tedious Routine usually followed at Water Cures.

H. McCALL, M. D., after a long and an extensive Practice—both in Acute and Chronic diseases—has evolved a mode of treatment by which he skillfully combines the use of Vapor Baths, Water Treatment, Electricity, Swedish Movements,

LIGHT AND HEAVY GYMNASTICS,

Rest, Recreation, Pure Air, Sunshine, a proper Dietary Regimen, Good Social Influences, etc., etc., and prescribing to each Patient such treatment as their individual cases merit; he quickly succeeds in breaking up Internal Congestions, rousing the system to expel effete and poisonous matter, and awakening the torpid or over-worked organs to renewed and healthy action. The Doctor never delays till to-morrow what can be done to-day, Nor does he compel Nature to perform without assistance the labor which should legitimately be done by the Physician. His Theory is to put the patient on the road to health at once by *Active Treatment*, and not be content with simple water treatment and waiting for months, and years, until struggling nature is *compelled* to make those violent and exhaustive efforts for the relief of the patient, which are familiarly known as *Crises*, and occur in the form of boils, rashes, eruptions, diarrhœas, fevers, flying pains, nervous prostration, restlessness, etc., etc. The Deterging Treatment is followed by as great an amount of active exercise as patients can bear without a waste of vitality, and they soon find themselves gaining in strength and weight; their old troubles gradually yield to normal conditions, prolapsed organs resume their natural positions; despondency and gloom give place to buoyancy of spirits, and they are enabled to return to their homes restored in health, restored to friends, to the world, to labor, and the demands of christianity. To be sick is a terrible misfortune! To be well, that we may labor, a glorious boon!

Young men, suffering from Nervous Debility, will find we possess advantages for their treatment not offered by any other Institution in the country. Special attention given to Female diseases—kind and competent lady-assistants always in attendance.

Our Gymnasium is furnished with a HYGEOMETER—a machine recently invented by Dr. LAWRENCE—that combines the essential properties for effecting a Perfect Physical Development which are offered by the machines of Dio Lewis, Windship, Butler, and Taylor respectively. ☞Orders solicited; can be forwarded by Express. Price--$45,00.

☞For our terms for Board and Treatment, and other information,
Address **H. McCALL, M. D.,**

Or, McCALL, MILLER & Co.   Galesburg, Ills.